FROM THE BARRIO TO WASHINGTON

From the Barrio to Washington

AN EDUCATOR'S JOURNEY

★ ★ ★ ★ ★

BY ARMANDO RODRIGUEZ

AS TOLD TO KEITH TAYLOR

University of New Mexico Press ★ Albuquerque

© 2007 by Armando Rodriguez and Keith Taylor
All rights reserved. Published 2007
Printed in the United States of America
10 09 08 07   1 2 3 4 5 6 7

Library of Congress Cataloging-in-Publication Data
Rodriguez, Armando, 1921–
From the barrio to Washington : an educator's journey /
by Armando Rodriguez as told to Keith Taylor.
p. cm.
Includes index.
ISBN-13: 978-0-8263-4381-9 (CLOTH : ALK. PAPER)
1. Rodriguez, Armando, 1921–
2. School principals—United States—Biography.
3. Hispanic American school principals—Biography.
4. Politicians—United States—Biography.
5. Hispanic American politicians—Biography.
I. Taylor, Keith, 1930– II. Title.
LA2317.R64A3 2007
370.92—dc22
2007027489

★

Special thanks to Bettie Baca for her editing.

Book and jacket design and typesetting by Kathleen Sparkes
This book is typeset using Sabon LT STD 10.5/14, 26P.
Display type is LinoLetter STD.

★

I WISH TO RECOGNIZE THE ENCOURAGEMENT,

INSPIRATION, AND EFFORTS OF

MR. RANDOLPH A. HEARST

AND THE SUPPORT PROVIDED BY THE

WILLIAM R. HEARST FOUNDATION

ON BEHALF OF BILINGUAL EDUCATION

IN THE UNITED STATES.

★

Contents

☆ ☆ ☆

Foreword

I got to know Armando Rodriguez well in 1962. Among the candidates in the usual half-dozen political races in San Diego County that year, I was running for Congress; he, for the state legislature. I came to think of Armando as the best qualified among all of us, present company included. Yet, while I was winning a hairline victory, Armando didn't quite make it.

And I think I know why. My name has a safely northern European ring to it, while *Rodriguez* is unmistakably Hispanic. Californians were not yet ready to elect a Hispanic.

As his timely autobiography makes clear, Armando's subsequent life—his endless succession of Hispanic "firsts"—has helped change things. California's present state government is replete with Garcias, Hernandezes, and Bustamantes. Enough of them represent districts of non-Hispanic majority to suggest that the old prejudices are done for.

If this is so, no one has contributed more to our state's rising level of maturity than the man whose friends call him Shadow. He didn't hear English spoken until he was six. And he endured many a put-down in a world he must often have felt was not meant for an undersized stranger—not even one endowed with the heart of a lion.

That he has made it—and made it big—in this new world speaks well for his ability. That he did it without ever feeling sorry for himself attests to the man's character.

And there's a supporting member of the cast—"The Girl from Across the Street." Associate biographer Keith Taylor puts a fifty-eight-year love affair and a strong woman's contribution to history in fascinating perspective.

I'm prouder than I can say to have known both.

Lionel Van Deerlin, member,
House of Representatives, 1962–80

Preface

They say life is a journey. If so, I haven't reached the station yet, but for all I know, it's just around the next corner. I don't want to go away without giving the many members of my extended family, my friends across the country, and everyone else some idea of just who old Tio Mando (Uncle Mando) was.

Sure that's egotistical, but it's also the prerogative of an old man—eighty-six years old on my last birthday. I just hope this story is interesting enough for folks to read. More importantly, I hope it inspires some youngster—inside or outside my family, Latino, black, or white—to keep on fighting to succeed when the odds against success are so great that the easiest course would be to give up.

I once lived in a small house with nine relatives, and my sleeping space was any unoccupied spot—often as not on the floor. I sold magazines and tamales door to door. I picked up chunks of ice from an ice plant in San Diego and beat the ice company's deliverymen to the door with cheaper ice.

Later I dined in the White House, met some of the world's most powerful people, and helped shape the future of my country and the world. I'm proud of all that, and I hope you can share my pride.

This is more than my life's story, though. It's our love story, Beatriz's and mine. More than half a century ago, Beatriz Serrano became my wife. Although it might have made a more exciting and salacious story if I'd had a succession of wives, she is still my wife. Bea was the one I wanted to marry. She's the one I've grown old with and the only wife I ever wanted.

If I have earned respect for any achievements, my lovely wife Bea deserves a lot of the credit.

I love her, and I dedicate *our* story to her.

FIGURE 1.
Andres Rodriguez
(Armando's father),
circa 1939.

The Early Years, 1921–34

What would be the odds of a poor Mexican boy, thirteenth kid in a family of fourteen, making it big in the rich country to the north?

Long odds? Oh, but they get longer than that. Let's say the kid was short and so dark he was called "Shadow." When he first stepped foot in the United States, he couldn't speak one word of English, and he was just old enough to start school, a school with few Spanish-speaking teachers.

That was me as a brand new immigrant. About the only things going for me were that Mom and Dad insisted I get an education and that I learned to work hard. Most anything can be overcome with a combination like that.

My knowledge of the history of my family is incomplete, but I do know that my life's journey started on September 30, 1921, in Gomez Palacio in Mexico's central valley, an area similar to California's Imperial Valley. I'd say the population was about fifteen thousand.

Dad's name was Andres Rodriguez. Mom's was Petra Cardenas. I was the seventh of eight living children; we think six others died. Our family history and official records from early twentieth-century central Mexico aren't complete.

I do know that my parents eloped when Dad was nineteen and Mom was fourteen. They did not even have a ceremony for several months, and then it was the one required by Mexican law, a civil ceremony. Later they satisfied their church's and government's requirements by being married in a religious ceremony.

I also know that my father was successful, or as successful as a person who was not well connected or wealthy could be in an agricultural

FIGURE 2. Left to right: Felicita Cardenas (Armando's grandmother), Silvestre Cardenas (Armando's grandfather),
and Petra Cardenas (Armando's mother), circa 1899.

section of a poor country. In his youth, he worked as a farmhand. Later Dad was a conductor on streetcars connecting Gomez Palacio, Durango, and Torreón. After that, he established a corner grocery store near our home in Gomez Palacio.

One thing's for sure: my dad always worked, whether it was in the United States or in Mexico. I learned a lot from him, but his most important legacy was his work ethic. It served me well throughout my life, even after I graduated from manual labor.

Mom wasn't really sure of all of her family's history, but she was sure her maternal grandfather was a well-known general in the Mexican army during the revolution. She was less sure of which side he fought on.

Poor, and descended from farmers, shopkeepers, and perhaps even generals, the Rodriguez and Cardenas families were close-knit. Even today they get together for family reunions complete with singing, dancing, eating, and reminiscing. It's a great tradition, and I'm so glad Beatriz and I still work hard to keep it alive.

I often reflect that I'd have remained a Mexican citizen except for Napoleonic law, a close-knit family, and fate. My father certainly didn't want to leave his native land. The workings of Mexican law are based on a precept of the Napoleonic code that held a person was guilty until proven innocent. If a charge was severe enough, the person charged might well wait in jail until he proved he wasn't guilty. Jail, especially a Mexican *cárcel*, is not a happy place, but a stay in jail was in the offing for my elder brother Encarnación, or Chon as we called him. Chon, an accountant at a local country club, was accused of misappropriating funds, and at that point he was considered guilty under Mexican law.

My father had to make a difficult decision. He decided to move practically his entire family from their native country to protect one of them. Thus, all of us except my eldest sister Hermila and her family headed to San Diego where, foreign country or not, we had relatives. Dad's two sisters and Mom's former sister-in-law lived in San Diego.

I remember little of the move that took place when I was a mere child, but I am positive we were legal immigrants because, these eighty years later, I still have the paper that says so. I keep it along with testimonials from presidents, governors, Congress members, cabinet officers, foreign leaders of all sorts, and other movers and shakers in my lifetime. I was a legal U.S. resident at age six, but I didn't become a citizen until many years later, when I was serving my new country as a soldier in its army.

My family, nine in all, was so large that we moved north in two shifts, each arriving by train. No welcoming committee. No hospitality wagon. We were on our own except for a couple of kind relatives. Aunt Cruz and her family of six put the nine of us up for a couple weeks. Then Aunt Valentina and her family of seven put us up for a few more weeks.

Today, if you go to Fourteenth and K, you'll see a San Diego bus-repair station, but if you had gone there in 1927, you'd have seen a small cottage. That cottage was our first home in the United States. At least it was the first place our family could call its own. It was unimpressive, so small that most of us had to search for a sleeping place that wasn't already occupied by another body. At bedtime, such spots were scarce. For all that, it was better than trying to have two large families in the same house.

Who else was on that corner? Beatriz Serrano, who would become the love of my life, was born there across the street some four years after I had arrived. There's a lot of sentiment for me today when I'm in the neighborhood of Fourteenth and K.

But, sentiments aside, in 1927 the cottage was just too small! After a couple months, we rented a real house, one with three bedrooms, a living room, a dining room, a bathroom, a garage, and a large yard. It was large enough for all of us to fit into if we held our breaths and squeezed. With more beds and a little imagination we usually got a good night's sleep.

And the yard! It was special for the Rodriguez family, but not because it was like something you'd see in *Home and Garden*. It wasn't; but for our large family, it had a more utilitarian function. Our yard was a place where we could heat water for washing clothes and bathing. Perhaps best of all, we converted part of it into a garden. And thank heaven for my father's experience in farming!

I was now in los Estados Unidos. I was ready for school, but I could not speak a bit of the language. That problem was partially corrected by the Abraham Lincoln Elementary School in a special class that taught me English. Little did I know then that I was coping with problems I would later try to solve on a much higher level. When, as an adult, I worked at the U.S. Office of Education, one of my duties was to fund and help establish bilingual education. I only had to look back to my childhood to find my motivation.

When I had conquered enough of my new language to handle subjects taught in English, I started kindergarten, but by this time I was seven. I could easily have skipped kindergarten, but my father wanted his children to have as much education as possible. Later, with the help of summer school, I skipped a grade.

Of course, education wasn't my family's only problem. Although we didn't have time to reflect on it, we were still poor. To this day, I can remember my mother cooking on an open set of burners, a primitive and dangerous way to cook.

With three kids—Catalina, Carlos, and I—in school, and the adults at work, life settled into a pattern that included family gatherings on weekends, an especially happy time for our clan. We made new friends. I especially remember our neighbors the Torrescanos—James and Emma and their five kids.

Isn't it funny how some childhood memories stick out? One incident caused no particular problems, but I remember it vividly. When I was eleven, some of us kids were playing cops and robbers with rubber-band guns, and I ran out in front of a car. Later I realized how horrified the driver must have been, but then all I knew was the pain of having my foot run over. Still, no lasting harm was done. I wore a cast for a while and that was it.

Of much more importance were two events occurring within about half a year. We lost two family members—Chon and Dad—and both were breadwinners. First, the country club in Mexico dropped all charges against Chon. (I'm guessing they found out who really stole the money.) Then the country club managers convinced a banana plantation to offer Chon an even better job than the one he had left behind six years earlier. The offer might have been an act of atonement, but it also must have served the plantation well, because they kept him on for about a dozen years. Later, Chon moved north to Tijuana so he could be closer to home but still remain in Mexico. He ended up as senior accountant at the Agua Caliente racetrack in Tijuana.

The loss of a second family member didn't turn out as well. It had its genesis in 1929 with the start of the greatest depression in American history. By 1931 our adopted country didn't want its own native-born citizens, especially the white ones, to have to compete with foreign people for jobs. To make matters worse, our adopted country wasn't particular how *foreign* was defined. Mexicans were easy targets. Some were, of course, here illegally. Many others, such as my father, were here legally. Yet others were U.S. citizens, supposedly with complete constitutional rights.

Little of that mattered to a desperate nation. According to *Decade of Betrayal*, a book by Francisco E. Balderrama and Raymond Rodríguez, official records from both Mexico and the United States showed more than a million Latinos were deported between 1931 and 1940. Were they all illegal immigrants? Not at all. Some 60 percent were native-born U.S. citizens!

Dad was one of the legal immigrants. Those years he was always looking for a job. One day, while standing in line for a construction job, he was approached by some government agents. They pulled him out of the line and had one of those infamous "heart-to-heart" talks with him. Their suggestion was that he'd be much better off in Mexico. The implication was obvious. Dad returned to Gomez Palacio.

Our family was now reduced to five, and we had only two wage earners. That isn't exactly correct. We *all* worked wherever we could make a buck. In desperate times, people take desperate measures. Mom and my eldest sister did piecework cleaning fish when the fishing boats came back full. As far back as I can remember, I tried to make a buck somehow. As we go along, I'll list the various jobs I had.

I'm not sure that working was all bad. Surely working and understanding the basic elements of economics are about the best hands-on experiences a kid can get. It's a whale of a lot better than watching endless cartoons on television. Whatever success I had in life was due more than anything to my early acquaintance with "sweat-of-the-brow" labor.

We kept moving, once to a smaller house in an alley. Then, when a vacancy materialized and our finances improved a bit, we moved to a larger house facing the street. This was part of life in Barrio Logan in the 1930s, and it wasn't much different from the rest of Depression-era America.

The Depression. Father expatriated to Mexico. It didn't really matter. The 1930s were hard times for everybody. I was growing up, playing, learning, and even having fun. Being poor was just a fact of life. Everybody was poor.

In the sixth grade, I learned something important: I wasn't dumb! For some reason, our teacher publicly told the entire class their IQs. I had the second highest in the class. Although uncalled for and probably harmful to some of the other kids, Mrs. Brown's act helped me indirectly. Understanding that I had brains helped sustain me whenever I felt like giving up.

Years later I learned I might not have been as smart as I had thought. When I was a visiting teacher at my former school, I looked up the old records. I confirmed my score but learned it wasn't an official test.

When I worked for the U.S. Department of Health, Education, and Welfare, a fellow worker invited me to join Mensa, but I declined. The guy wanted money, and I had better things to do with mine. I surely could show people my ability to think without having a piece of paper to back it up. Probably it was just as well that I didn't join the elite group of high-IQ folks. *Mensa* could be mistaken for the Mexican word *menso* (dummy). Hey, life would have been hell if my old buddies had been given an easy shot at me like that.

In an ironic twist, years later I saw that fellow's name in the papers. He had been arrested for soliciting a prostitute in the Washington DC area. Perhaps he wasn't so smart. He was one of the few who got caught at that.

In any case, I always reminded myself that hard work and perseverance beat sheer brain power any day. I'll stick with that and urge others to keep plugging away, whether they are Mensa members or mensos.

Our section of town was officially named Logan Heights. We Americans of Mexican heritage called it Barrio Logan, *barrio* being the Spanish-speaking district of a city. Despite living in Barrio Logan, my childhood friends were an eclectic group. Their names reflected northern European ancestry as well as Spanish and Mexican. I remember playing with kids named McGuire, Tucker, Johnson, and Valentine, as well as others named Fuentes, Marquis, and Luján.

I wonder if I'd have been able to serve my government as well as I did, if I hadn't learned to see things from the perspective of others so early in my life. Indeed, would I have learned English as well as I did? I had learned the basics of English at Abraham Lincoln Elementary, but it was playing with Jimmy McGuire that made it work. In turn, Jimmy learned Spanish as spoken in central Mexico, and he adapted to the idiom of the barrio of San Diego.

I feel sorry for folks who "stick to their own kind." They miss so much.

CHAPTER TWO

Junior and Senior
High School, 1934–40

MEMORIAL JUNIOR HIGH

Life's journey is just one adventure after the other, each tinged with the nagging suspicion that the next will be overwhelming. I have had a lifetime of those challenges. Some I conquered; some I didn't. But mostly I'm satisfied. I'm also certain the challenges will continue, and I'm relying on education and experience to cope with them—especially now that I'm eighty-six and unable to outrun the more challenging ones.

School is touted to be a preparation for adult life. It is, of course, but it's more than that—it is a metaphor for adult life. Both contain the fear of the unknown and the awe of those above us in the hierarchy. Has there ever been a kid in the first grade who didn't look at those big guys in the second and third grades and ask himself, "Will I ever be as smart as they are?" And as we move into junior high and then senior high, the ante is raised even higher. Puberty, machismo, and girls are mysteries all. And, at first, all seem unsolvable.

I don't want to do the "Oh, but you should have seen what it was like in my day" thing, but many things *were* different. Some were better, others worse. But they were different. Let me share those years with you.

But first, a disclaimer: I didn't walk uphill both ways through a raging blizzard to go to school. My sister Catalina and I walked to Memorial Junior High, now Memorial Academy. It was right there on Logan Avenue, an easy jaunt from our home. And instead of blizzards, we had weather typical of San Diego. Now and then we'd get wet in a rainstorm—at least local folks called it a storm. For a real rainstorm, one should take a stroll through Recife, Brazil, in the rainy season.

One thing that hasn't changed since I was a child is that kids don't bother with political correctness. Kids of all races—and my school comprised mostly Anglos, Negroes, and Latinos—were quick to hang nicknames on people based on their looks or ethnicity. It was so long ago that I forgot who did it, but someone hung the moniker *Shadow* on me.

It was a derogatory nickname given to me because I was even darker than the other kids of Mexican heritage. For all that, it didn't bother me much. I simply accepted it as something that couldn't be changed, and it stuck with me. Even a president was fascinated by my nickname. Long after I left school, Lyndon Johnson asked me about it. He was amused by the answer, but that was Lyndon.

In common with public schools across the country, in elementary school (kindergarten through sixth grade) we had one teacher who taught all the classes in just one room. But we looked ahead and knew things would be different. Those big kids in junior high had different teachers for different subjects, and we would move from room to room. We would have the brand new experience of six classes in different rooms, each with a different teacher. After a lifetime of experiences as an educator on many different levels, I realize it wasn't a big deal, but to a kid looking forward, it was one of the mysteries of life.

Ironically, eating—a subject my sister and I excelled in—looked to be one of our biggest problems at first. Of course, everybody in school ate, but everybody did not eat tacos. Mom would pack leftovers from the previous night's supper for our school lunch, and Mom's cuisine featured tacos. The other kids usually ate sandwiches, so, like kids everywhere, they made fun of somebody who did something different.

My sister and I solved that by sitting *under* the lunch table to eat our lunches. (As if that wouldn't attract attention!) Peeking under the table to see what the two Mexican kids were doing down there, the other kids would taunt us. We offered one of them a taco; he exchanged a sandwich for it. Of course, Mom's tacos were good. I think the sandwiches were also. At least they were a welcome change.

That may have been my first foray into politics, perhaps international relations. A little problem in southeast San Diego was headed off by food. It led to more variety in the diets of two cultures and made us new friends in the bargain. That was better than a taco or a bologna sandwich.

Mom interrupted that phase of our cultural indoctrination by changing our lunch to sandwiches. Sometimes good things come to an end too soon.

In grade school, I learned that although I was smart, I wasn't a genius. In junior and senior high I learned that although I was athletic, I wasn't a star. Still, when I took part in organized sports I found I had good coordination and was able to compete well, even though I was shorter than most of the other kids.

As a student, teacher, administrator, and public servant in Sacramento and Washington DC, I always wrestled with the proper place for athletics in our schools, especially high school and college. Exercise is important and is becoming more so every year. A 2004 study by Duke University told us that nearly 16 percent of our twelve- to nineteen-year-olds are obese. In the past, we didn't think much about that. Now it is something we cannot ignore any longer. Exercise is vital in fighting what *USA Today* called an epidemic.

But when we think of athletics and schools, we usually think of varsity games with all the pageantry and hoopla, and they are important too. No administrator would dare to de-emphasize the teams we so plaintively urge to "fight on." Old grads proudly hang on to their teams' nicknames: Cavers, Patriots, Barons, Aztecs, Trojans—even Banana Slugs. Furthermore, team sports, if taught properly, introduce young men and women to a concept of discipline often lacking in other endeavors.

Of course I wasn't thinking of all that when I tried out for track at San Diego High. I just wanted to belong to a team and beat somebody. Unfortunately track was the wrong sport. I wasn't fast enough at any distance, and my attempts at throwing the shot put were equally futile. I didn't beat anybody to speak of, and I wasn't even good enough to make the team.

Wrestling, though, was right down my alley, and it was so democratic because of the weight divisions. I didn't have to tackle some behemoth from Iowa; I simply had to beat other kids who weighed about the same as I did. Frank Crosby, the coach, saw enough potential in me that he encouraged me, and I ended up on the team, wrestling in the 125- or 128-and-under division. I did well too; I lost only one match during my final two years of high school.

The lessons of competitive sports have stood me in good stead all my life. Education isn't limited to what we learn from books.

I love competitive sports, in or out of school. I even became a boxer of sorts. Several of us would hang around the Coliseum over at Fifteenth and G Streets. There we watched the boxers and got to know some of them. We were also able to practice sparring, and we picked up a few pointers from the regular boxers. They even let us clean up the place!

All that led to my short-lived career as a boxer. After a few years of just hanging around, I wrangled an invitation to box as an amateur, although there was a small—very small—amount of prize money. I entered four bouts and won every one. When I learned that the prize money would make me ineligible for high school sports, I quit.

But my record stood until I was in the army. I was undefeated, and I would have stayed that way if someone hadn't talked me into again putting on the gloves.

One of my friends in the Catholic Youth Organization (the CYO), Manuel Monteverde, was a very good baseball player. He helped the rest of us learn the fundamentals of our national pastime. I learned them well enough to enjoy the game. Unfortunately, stardom in baseball wasn't to be. If a grandson or great grandson of mine turns into a Fernando Valenzuela, I can assume his prowess comes from the Serrano side of the family.

Perhaps some scion of mine will make it big as a football player. I played on the formidable Beardsley Street Bears, so named because we often played on Beardsley, a suitably unpaved street. We kids from the barrio played mostly among ourselves in the evenings. I don't remember our record, but I'm sure we were a tremendous team.

FIGURE 3. Our Lady of Guadalupe Church in San Diego, as it was in Armando's youth and when he and Beatriz were married.

I was also an altar boy at Our Lady of Guadalupe, that church you can see right off Interstate 5. Being an altar boy led to my membership in the Catholic Youth Organization. Again, many of my activities revolved around athletics, and the CYO sponsored many of them.

Still, school occupied most of my life, and it carries so many memories. Today a big park adjoins Memorial Academy. It has a gymnasium, a pool, a picnic area, and a Boys and Girls Club. Back in the early thirties, it was an undeveloped area. The kids called it "the Forty Acres," although it fell far short of forty acres.

The area was used by angry students to seek revenge for some insult, slur, or slight. There were no rules. The pair would just square off and have at it. In spite of all my ability in becoming an undefeated boxer, I never tested my prowess as a brawler in the Forty Acres.

I'm glad the battlefield has been replaced by a park. Nostalgia aside, I see little good in kids fighting. Fighting usually accomplishes nothing. Come to think of it, that goes for countries as well as kids, something I wish my country would think of more often.

On a more peaceful note, one special event was Memorial's annual gala pageant, *The Passing Review*. Appropriately enough, the drama teacher was in charge. When I was in the ninth grade, my last year of junior high, the theme was "Dana Days in San Diego." "Dana" referred to Richard Henry Dana Jr., author of *Two Years Before the Mast*.

I landed the coveted role of an Indian doing a war dance. I'm sure I was a smashing success. Acting wild and warlike came naturally to me at that age. The director that year was Dr. Sue Earnest, who later became my mentor at San Diego State.

That was not the only organized dancing I took part in. Dancing was a special subject we were taught so that at the end of junior high, we could actually dance with girls! That was, of course, met with misgivings by thirteen- and fourteen-year-olds of both sexes.

Years later I was a teacher at Memorial Junior High. Guess what was one of the subjects I taught? Yep, dancing, and I was pretty good at it too, thanks to Dr. Earnest.

Soon I was old enough for high school. From the perspective of a kid in Memorial Junior High, those guys over in San Diego High School were gods. Would I ever be able to make it through such a place?

Of course, like almost all such bugaboos, the mystery of high school simply vanished once I walked through the front door. Far from being arcane rituals, daily routines were really similar to those in junior high. We went into the subjects more deeply, of course, and I had to balance study time with everything else that went on in my life as a teenager.

One thing that didn't vanish when I entered high school was that Shadow was still in a world run by Anglos. On the entire faculty, there was only one Latino teacher. People like me did not participate in the glee club, the school band, theater, Associated Student Body Council, student court, Boys Federation, Girls League, or the school newspaper.

We Latinos wanted to feel like we also belonged. In institutions everywhere, there is always one person who seems to know the answer to everything. In San Diego High School, it was Jack Hoxie, who was an Anglo and a jock. He worked part time in the business office. When I was a junior, I approached him about the problem of Latinos not feeling like they belonged at the high school.

Jack was more than willing to help, and he had a great idea. He suggested we form a club that would serve the needs of Latinos. Not only that, he helped organize it and gave all sorts of advice on how to get it going.

Following Jack's advice, we proudly started El Club Amigable, the friendly club. I am proud that I was an organizer and the first president. Unfortunately, the word *amigable* wasn't embraced by the English-speaking students and faculty. So El Club Amigable became the "Gobble Gobble Club." That stung, but we persevered.

El Club Amigable organized successful events such as conferences about how we Latinos contributed to the school and community. We also honored our heritage by sponsoring fiestas on Mexican holidays. We reached out to the rest of the school and invited everybody, but El Club Amigable was mostly for ourselves.

Alas, the Gobble Gobble Club story didn't end with it having changed the entire school, and I'm to blame as much as anybody. By the time I was a senior, I was so involved in schoolwork, jobs, senior activities, athletics, and my social life, that I left our club behind.

But the club was a great idea, and I'm glad I was a part of it. Lessons I learned from it became the basis for ideas I implemented during my career in education. My friendship with Jack Hoxie was also a good idea. I would hear from him again some seventeen years later.

When I was in the tenth grade, I went out for class B football, which was limited to smaller and generally younger guys. I did stick with the sport until I was injured in my senior year, and that was it for football. Although I was first-string varsity, I never became a football star (except perhaps with the Beardsley Street Bears).

Football led to track and wrestling. And wrestling introduced me to coach Frank Crosby. Coach Crosby showed me how to be a good sport, something hard to do in any sort of fighting, but especially hard when you're grappling with a guy who is trying to immobilize you.

Our coach encouraged me to do two things that are antithetical to wresting: help others and be kind. Coach was not only my teacher, but he also became a very good friend. I'll never forget his lessons; I cannot overemphasize his influence on my life.

Coach and I corresponded regularly, and we exchanged visits. He came to Sacramento and Washington to visit us, and I visited him in his hometown of Saint George, Utah. We kept in touch until he died about fifteen years ago.

Ironically, Coach Crosby's being kind came back to haunt him in a way. He was a teacher who was a hero to so many students. Long after our high school years, the Henson brothers—a couple of my teammates on the San Diego High wrestling team—visited with our old coach when he came by my house on his way to visit a sister in Connecticut. At the time I was working at the Department of Health, Education, and Welfare, and the Hensons were colonels in the army.

The three of us took Coach Crosby to the train station for his return trip home. As happens so often with kind people, someone took advantage of him. A young man, with others hanging out nearby, approached him and "accidentally" dropped a bag of coins. When Coach stopped to help him, the other kids grabbed his wallet and ran. His friends, the Hensons and I, gave him money to make it back to Saint George.

It's appropriate that this was the guy who coached me, indeed the entire team, in the sport where we could excel. We won the league championship (the league covered all of southern California) in my senior year. I did my part by winning my weight class of 128 pounds for high school wrestling and 125 pounds for the Amateur Athletic Association. I even wrestled over my weight class in both, and we won both weights at the state championships.

I've been asked for details about my wrestling, but I don't really have any. I do know that the sport requires so much mental discipline that my toughest opponent was me myself. Coach Crosby instilled that idea in me. The result was that I lost only twice in all of my matches, and those losses were when I inadvertently let up. Twice was two times too many.

I survived, perhaps thrived on, the rigors of high school, and in June of 1940 I was among the six hundred proud San Diego High School students who gathered to receive diplomas in the organ pavilion of Balboa Park. I'll never forget the moment when I stepped forward, shook the hand of the school superintendent, and moved my tassel from the left side to the right side of my cap. I was now a high school graduate, but I was not yet a citizen of my adopted country.

FIGURE 4. Armando at graduation from San Diego
High School, 1940.

Yes, the Tio Mando of today was shaped by my school days, but not only by the school and its environment. I was also shaped by the people I knew there. I hate to burden a reader with a list of names, but this is my history, and these guys are so much a part of it I simply won't leave them out. And my apologies to those who have slipped my mind.

Perhaps one of the most interesting fellows I knew in school was Manuel Calles. We met because he was interested in joining El Club Amigable. He not only joined, he also became a good friend—and he was a good guy to be friends with.

Manuel was a handsome dude, so handsome that the girls flocked to him. A good friend of a popular guy like that got pretty lucky himself sometimes. But Manuel's, and to a lesser extent, my, popularity might have come from more than his looks: he was one of the few kids who had his own car. In fact, I'll bet he was the only guy at San Diego High in the late thirties to have a brand new one—a spiffy 1939 Hudson convertible with big white sidewall tires.

He and I tooled around in that big car all over town for about four months. Then he disappeared. All we had to go on was a rumor that he had "got a girl in trouble and his father sent him away."

You had to figure his father ran things with an iron hand. At the insistence of my friend, I met this man, but only briefly. Manuel was very proud of his dad, who I learned was an important man indeed. His name was Plutarco Elías Calles, and he was president of Mexico from 1924 to 1928. Furthermore, he is considered by many historians to have effectively controlled the country for six years after he was president.

From the point of view of a resident of the United States, where freedom of religion is jealously guarded, the history of this president of my native land is an especially interesting one. In 1926 President Calles signed what has become known as Calles's Law. It prohibited clergy and others from wearing church garb—even decorations. The punishment was a fine of five hundred pesos, and up to five years in prison, even for just questioning the law. The law still stands.

For this and other actions that didn't suit a Catholic country, Plutarco Calles and nine of his collaborators were deported in 1936. He moved to San Diego, but not to the barrio. The Calles family lived in the fanciest house I'd ever been in, and it was in a section of town where I seldom ventured.

All of that history was more interesting after I got involved in American politics, and it is even more interesting now that I look back on it from the perspective of an old man with an ever-increasing interest in his native land. But at the time, the antics with the younger Calles and his much younger car took all my attention.

I also hung around with Alfred Salazar, Alex Le Grand, Alfred Beauloye, and Preston Maupin (who didn't like to be called Preston, so that's what we called him). Then there were Jimmy Murgia, Joe Sussetti, Fernando Paredes, and Duane Pillette. Most of these guys and I played baseball on the Leu Hardware team. A few even became members of the American Legion baseball championship team.

In the barrio I hung out with the Delgadillo brothers—Gregory, Jesús, and Joe—and with a couple of kids with the Anglo sounding name Keniston—Frank and Jimmy. Then there were Edgar Azhochar, Andy Canales, Phil Ybarra, Salvador Bringas, Frank León, and Augustine "Red" Gonzales, who later became a Trappist monk.

All this time I was trying to perfect my English. It wasn't easy when talking to kids who had Spanish as their first language.

For all that, education is never restricted to what folks learn in schools. One of the most important things I learned was how to make money, an essential lesson in a large family with a limited amount of the stuff. I suspect that if more of our politicians had the experience of having to work for a living, we would be governed more wisely.

Few experiences serve youth better than working for money, especially when ingenuity is required. And ingenuity is required when a kid is competing with adults for a buck, or in those days, a few cents. That was my case when, as a little boy, I sold large chunks of ice door to door. Rather than buy it wholesale, I would pick up chunks of broken ice from the warehouse floor and sell them at a huge discount, often to homes that displayed an "Ice Wanted" sign that had been placed there by the regular deliveryman.

It was a good gig as long as it lasted, and it lasted until the regular ice salesmen found out about it. Then it was all over. Ingenuity can carry a fellow just so far.

Like kids all across America during the Depression, I worked throughout my school years. Tia Valentina made great tamales, and my sisters and I sold them door to door, but with limited success. I suspect tamales weren't all that unique in a neighborhood filled with Mexican Americans, or Mexicans as we were called then. I have to concede that it's likely that other kids' aunts also made great tamales.

I also remember that one of our neighbors had a bumper crop of lemons. She suggested we sell the lemons and split the cost. We did, and actually made some money at it.

I graduated to magazines and sold a bunch of them, including *Liberty, Saturday Evening Post, Woman's Home Companion,* and *Country Gentleman.*

My stint selling papers was a Horatio Alger story, but on a much smaller scale. I was first a newsboy for the now long-defunct *San Diego Sun.* It wasn't easy though; the *Sun* never threatened either the *Union* or the *Tribune* (they were separate papers then) as top-selling papers in San Diego. In addition, I was assigned a lousy corner where few prospective customers showed up. I switched to a better-selling paper, *The Los Angeles Examiner.* And I had a better corner. Things went so well I made enough money to buy a bicycle. After that, I graduated to a real paper route for the *San Diego Union.*

Over the years, I did anything to make a buck. A boat's whistle would summon kids to the dock to clean mackerel. That was piecework of course, so it behooved us to learn to clean the slippery things efficiently. I answered many a whistle and cleaned many a smelly mackerel. So did my sister Catalina, and it paid off for her. She later held a very influential position as the workers' representative for the CIO (Congress of Industrial Organizations) Fish Cannery Workers Union.

My experiences with cultural diversity, which have been so valuable to me my entire life, paid off early. Some Filipino friends got me a job at Casa De Mañana, a four-star restaurant in La Jolla. For a kid, especially one who was the only non-Filipino in the kitchen, that was a coveted job.

I don't remember a lot of things I learned in school, but I haven't forgotten any of the lessons I learned while earning money. And one of the biggest things I took from working, especially selling English-language newspapers, is that I had to learn how to use the language of my adopted country effectively. Selling, especially to folks with a different skin color than mine, helped me hone my language skills and gave me the confidence I needed to work in my adopted country.

I suppose, like so many kids, I disliked school at the time, but when I look back, those years were the most important years of my life. And the memories are all good ones.

No. They are wonderful ones!

CHAPTER THREE

An Immigrant, an Emigrant, and a Soldier, 1940–43

The word *tween* is a contraction of the old English word *betwene*. It dates back to the thirteenth century, and it may be nautical in origin. San Diego's stellar tourist attraction is the aptly named barque *Star of India*. Also aptly named is the first deck down, the tween deck. It is so named because it's a half deck between the main deck and the first full deck.

I wasn't seven centuries old, nautical, or English, but *tween* certainly described me in 1940. I had graduated from San Diego High in June, and I was on my way to becoming whatever a Mexican kid who had immigrated to the rich country to the north would become if he had boundless ambition, but only a high school education and limited work experience.

RETURN TO GOMEZ PALACIO

At age nineteen, I wasn't even a citizen of the rich country where I had lived, gone to school, and worked for thirteen years. And it started to look as if I might never be. Mexico was always home to my father. After his forced exile, he had managed to return to the United States, but he wasn't happy here. He wanted to go home, and home was still Gomez Palacio.

He wanted to take his children who were still at home with him. We were certainly old enough to refuse, and we did consider it, but our father wanted us all to go so badly. He was a good father, but he could also be quite hardheaded. He was adamant, so we finally accepted his idea that it would be good for all of us to move. I would go on to college; Catalina would get a job; Carlos, only fifteen, would continue with school. We would be in Mexico where we belonged.

Thus, a short month after my graduation from high school, five of us reversed our trip of 1927. Dad, Mom, Catalina, Carlos, and I made the trip. The others either already lived in Mexico or stayed in San Diego. As I remember it, we took the Southern Pacific to El Paso. Then we crossed the border at Juárez, and caught the Ferrocarrile Nacionales to Gomez Palacio.

We kids tried to be optimistic. We even convinced ourselves that moving back was a good idea. After all, we did have a plan. Planning is half the battle, isn't it? But it wasn't long before we realized that the plan wasn't working. My San Diego barrio Spanish was quite different from that spoken in Gomez Palacio. It was not good enough for me to enter college. I would have needed additional classes to even start in a Mexican college. Catalina, thanks to her good knowledge of English, could get a job, but the pay was far too low to amount to much. Poor Carlos learned he was just too Americanized for Gomez Palacio. He would have to enroll in a special class to learn enough Spanish to even make it in a Mexican secondary (high) school.

In Mexico, we were all *tweeners*, just as we had been in San Diego. On the one hand, up there we were often shut out of mainstream American teenage life. On the other hand, we had made friends in the United States and had adapted to the place. To make it worse, I, like Carlos, had language problems in Mexico.

Our "good idea" of returning to Mexico turned out to be not so good after all. Even Dad and Mom reluctantly agreed with us. We would go back north, but it wouldn't be easy. Although we had lived thirteen years in the United States, we didn't have automatic freedom to return. The governments of two nations had their own red tape that we had to overcome.

Rather than just pack up and leave, we had to get permission from the Mexican government. Then the United States required us to get letters of recommendation for employment, obtain evidence we would not be dependent on the government, and show we had a place to live. And we needed money—lots of it. We scrimped and saved and borrowed and begged. It took a while, but the approval happened. In fact, I'm amazed it happened as fast as it did, considering all the problems we had to overcome.

I look back in wonder and gratitude to the many family members in Mexico and the United States who made so many sacrifices to make us Americans.

AND BACK TO THE UNITED STATES

On Lincoln's birthday, February 12, 1941, our family returned to San Diego. We were home! For Carlos, Catalina, and me, the idea of living in Mexico as Mexicans would never again enter our minds, or so we thought. Much later, after I'd retired from public service, I thought differently, but that's a story for later.

When we returned to San Diego that February in early 1941, it was almost as if we had never moved away. We rented a house only a block from the one we had left the previous June. As always, we all chipped in to work and make ends meet. Dad's efforts were hampered by his limited use of the English language. He worked in construction; he also worked in the fish cannery and anywhere else he could find employment. Even I, with my American education and better command of the language, was above him in the pecking order, but still not far from the bottom of the heap. With the help of some old childhood friends, I got a job in a laundry. Then I moved up, but not by much. I got a job at the fish cannery where I'd worked earlier. At least it was steady work, and it paid better than the laundry.

With the combined efforts of all of us, we got along relatively well. I even managed to improve my social life a bit. I went to dances and movies. I wrestled at the Neighborhood House. And like all young guys, sometimes I just hung out on the corner.

THE COMING WAR

In 1941 the sports activities were improving as the armed forces were expanding. The extra sailors, coast guardsmen, marines, and soldiers meant more competition for our baseball teams.

Athletic competition wasn't the only thing changing in 1941. San Diego was breaking away from its moorings of being a medium-sized, sleepy navy town and becoming a boisterous major player in the second war to end all wars. In early 1941, World War II had not yet come to America, but—with the possible exception of those at Pearl Harbor—we all knew it was on the way.

The population of San Diego in 1941 was just under 150,000. Then it started growing more rapidly than any city in the country. In a short time, its population jumped from 200,000 to over 300,000. Few among today's 1,223,402 San Diego residents would recognize my hometown of the early 1940s.

Not everything was different, of course. San Diego was then, even more than now, a navy and Marine Corps town. Many of the stations and bases are much the same now as they were six decades ago—the Marine Corps boot camp, Naval Air Station North Island, Miramar Navy (now Marine) Air Station, and the naval station (then destroyer base) stretching north and south of Thirty-second Street. Others, such as the naval training center on Rosecrans and the navy radio-transmitting station at Chollas Heights with its blinking aircraft-warning lights, have disappeared.

And San Diego had army posts in those days. They were significant then and became more significant when we went to war. Camp Lockett near Campo was the home of the now legendary Buffalo Soldiers. They weren't so legendary then, being "Negroes" and all, but they were a proud outfit dating back to just after the Civil War, when they served primarily in buffalo country. Later Camp Lockett was home to quite another sort of soldier: German and Italian prisoners of war.

I wonder how many golfers at the famous Torrey Pines Course or how many professors at the University of California, San Diego, realize they are playing golf or thinking profound thoughts where Camp Callan, a huge artillery training camp, once stood. There have been more changes of course, but I just wanted to give the reader a feel for the town where I started my adult life. That sleepy little sailor town down by Mexico was taking a giant leap into the future of a highly technical and mechanized America.

Meanwhile, my life was improving. In fact, it was pretty good. As Dad liked to say, "my plate was full," not a bad metaphor for a young man whose plate had not always been full. In addition to everything else, I spent quite a bit of time with church activities, helping out with the Catholic Youth Organization and coaching various teams. I was enjoying life and would have been content except for one thing.

My determination to live the American dream included a college education. I kept that in mind all the time. And am I glad I did! I'm sure an autobiography of a fish cleaner would not have served as an inspiration to anybody, even if I could make it interesting.

Meanwhile, my adopted country was getting geared up for the war. I was old enough to enlist, and I probably would have except for one thing: I still was not a citizen in the country where I had lived for so long. Ironically, it was the army that helped me to become a citizen. But my citizenship didn't "just happen"; it was the result of a long chain of events. After Pearl Harbor, I had to register for the draft despite the fact that I couldn't enlist because I wasn't a citizen. In a move typical of the bureaucracy of two governments, I was given the choice of signing up for the draft here or in Mexico. Because I had already decided that I wouldn't live in Mexico as a citizen again, I opted for the U.S. Army.

Then, on December 7, 1941, everything changed. The war we had been expecting for so long had arrived—at least in Pearl Harbor, a mere 2,600 miles away. That's closer than Boston is to San Diego, and there was practically nothing between Hawaii and San Diego to stop Japan. Our fleet had been destroyed, and distance meant little in a conflict that was fought around the globe. Suddenly, war was real.

Most people alive then can remember exactly what they were doing when they heard the news about Pearl Harbor. I was ready to head to Our Lady of Guadalupe for Mass when I heard about it. I rounded up three of my friends—Leonard and Manuel Fierro and Victor Negrete. Together we sat around the kitchen table at the Fierro house and discussed the future. Indeed, we wondered if we would have much of a future after all.

IN THE ARMY

I was twenty years old but would soon be twenty-one. What then? I decided to help fate decide my future. On September 30, 1942, my twenty-first birthday, I applied for U.S. citizenship. The army also helped a bit. Uncle Sam pointed his finger at me and said, "I want you." I was drafted even though I couldn't volunteer.

Heeding Uncle Sam's call, I reported for induction on December 15, took a bus about a hundred miles north to Fort McArthur in San Pedro, and became Private Armando Rodriguez, U.S. Army, SIR! Then I went home for Christmas, thinking if that was all there was to it, this army business would be a snap.

It wasn't, of course. The day after Christmas, I reported back to Fort McArthur, where I had some tests and received so many injections that my arm was sore for days. All that, and I had no idea what sort of duty awaited me.

The army wanted this bilingual young man with expertise in bussing tables and cleaning mackerel to work in the Signal Corps. Perhaps those tests revealed some talent I didn't know I had. At any rate, I was off to Camp Kohler, a Signal Corps training camp near Sacramento. If nothing else, I was seeing the world—or California, anyway.

There was more soldiering to be learned. The army taught me how to disassemble my rifle, reassemble it, clean it, and fire it. We recruits became good—well, pretty good—at close-order drill, and we went on long marches. We learned how to drive Jeeps and two-ton trucks in convoys. It was new, interesting, and adventuresome. I was surprised at how much new stuff could be crammed into my head in a short time.

Sports, as always, were of interest to me. When I learned that the camp had a boxing team, I joined. After all, I was undefeated, and I figured to get even better. We had a coach named Sergeant Reyes, who had been a professional featherweight boxer in Los Angeles.

My perfect record was broken when I got whupped in a decision, but I won my other fight. And that was it for boxing. My record stands at five of six, and considering that I'm eighty-six years old, that record probably won't change.

In January 1943 the army sent me to a part of the country where I would spend a lot of time later—the East. Fort George G. Meade, Maryland, is halfway between our nation's capital and Baltimore. It was, and still is, a huge army post. It would be my home for about six months, but it wouldn't be a warm, cozy one. Maryland is a cold place in winter, especially to a young man who was born in central Mexico and who had barely discovered cool weather in balmy San Diego.

Thanks, perhaps, to the luck of the draw or to a high score on some sort of aptitude test, my army life would not be one of toting a rifle and sleeping in the mud. I was assigned to the 837th Signal Company, and I had an important job: getting fast and accurate information to units going into battle. I doubt a person can overestimate how important that was. I sent and received messages by different means—telephone, teletype, radio, and what we now call snail mail. I had to learn how to process them all.

But it wasn't all training and work. It seemed that everybody was in the army, and a lot of the army was at Fort Meade. I ran into old friends from home. I found Lazaro "Larry" Lupian, a kid I'd hung out with in Logan Heights. I also made contact with another hometown friend, Johnny Remley, who was stationed at nearby Aberdeen Depot in Baltimore.

The nation's capital was just down the road about thirty-five miles. Although I was far away from home in a world I'd never seen before, I was able to visit Washington, never dreaming that someday I'd be one of the guys working there, making things happen.

But none of those—the training, the sightseeing, or even meeting old friends—was the most important thing that happened to me at Fort Meade. The most important thing was that I became a U.S. citizen. It came about almost as an accident.

Much of the information that comes through message centers is classified, and some of it has to be decoded. Part of my training involved simple cryptography, but learning it required a security clearance.

One day I was hard at work on a problem, when I sensed someone behind me. I glanced back and saw my commanding officer. He asked, "Did you know that material you are studying is classified, and is to be seen only by U.S. citizens?"

"No sir," I replied. "But I have lived in the United States since I was six and have applied for citizenship. A copy of my request is in my records."

You could almost see the wheels turning in his head. After a while he ordered, "Private Rodriguez, return to the barracks until we figure out what to do about this."

Back to the barracks I went. Although those documents were safe from my eyes, I would be unable to carry out the simplest of my duties without a clearance. Soon, however, I was ordered to change into my dress uniform and wait. In a little while, my commanding officer came by in a Jeep, picked me up, and drove me to Baltimore. He had found a federal judge who could swear me in as a brand new U.S. citizen. The army would not be thwarted in its efforts to turn me into a decoder of things classified.

I was a little disappointed that I became a citizen without any fanfare. The ceremony was done by a somewhat bored judge. There were no parades, no bands, no grandiose speeches, and there was only one flag alongside the judge's bench. But on June 6, 1943, just one year before D-Day, I finally belonged to, and belonged in, the country that I had grown up in and had sworn to defend.

In late June, the 837th Signal Company was sent to New Orleans before being shipped overseas. During our brief stopover, we got to see the French Quarter—Bourbon Street and all. We had an exciting time, but I'll say no more about it than that.

Then, after stops in Guantánamo Bay, Cuba, and Belém and Natal, Brazil, we arrived at our destination, Recife, Brazil. In Recife, the U.S. Army Air Force shuttled bombers and transports carrying equipment to North Africa, where Americans had been fighting since Operation Torch began on November 8, 1942. My job would be to provide communications support for those planes.

Of all the countries in South America, I landed in one of the few where Spanish was not the official language. Brazil had once been a colony of Portugal. Portuguese had many similarities to my native tongue, but the words sounded different, probably because, like French, they all seemed to be pronounced through the nose. Learning this language would be another challenge for me.

Our first stop was A Cidade de Nossa Senhora do Belém do Gran Para, more generally known as Belém. Belém (Portuguese for Bethlehem) is the largest city in northern Brazil, and it sits at the confluence of the Para estuary and the mighty Amazon. I immediately commenced learning a new language at the City of Our Lady of Bethlehem by the Grand River.

Then at our next stop, Natal, I got more language practice by working alongside Brazilian laborers loading and unloading our ship. It was not only good language practice, it was a good way to learn the vernacular of the common people. That suited a guy from the barrio just fine. I had no problem relating to folks who actually toiled for a living.

Then we went on to Recife, where I was assigned to the message center. I would finally be able to carry out my duties. All that training the army put into me would pay off.

And it did—for about two weeks. Then I had a recurrence of a problem I'd been plagued with since my early days in the army—a mucous buildup that made me hack and cough. But this time, I just couldn't shake it off like I did the previous attacks. I went to sick call, and a nurse thought I had malaria. The doctor examined me and sent me to the hospital. After a week I got better and I was given some medication and sent back to my company for light duty.

Not long after that, I was summoned to report to the commanding officer. Every soldier knows that can't be good news, and this wasn't. The nervous young captain told me that my mother had died, and that the army would send me home on something called bereavement leave.

He arranged for me to hitch rides on U.S. Army Air Force planes all the way home. Getting to San Diego from Recife, Brazil, wasn't easy, not in war time. The cities are more than six thousand miles apart as the crow flies. I zigzagged across the country, trying to get home. After a succession of flights, I arrived home—three days after Mom had been buried.

I had a strong and supportive family. We were able to share our grief, and the unity helped. So did the warm memories of our mother, a woman who lived in two countries and two centuries.

I can't let this chapter go by without talking a bit about this wonderful woman who did her best in a difficult time. Doña Petra was a great mom who had raised eight children over a period of twenty-five years. She did it with no formal education. She wasn't able to speak the language of the country where she lived most of her life, and she wasn't even able to read in her native language.

But, despite those handicaps, Mom did her very best. She was a working mom in every sense. She cleaned fish at the cannery and cleaned houses on her days off from the cannery. She was truly a great

FIGURE 5. Private First Class Armando Rodriguez, 1944.

mom, but by the time she was fifty-nine years old, she was tired, and she needed rest. I hope she realized what a great family she had raised. That was always so important to her.

While I was home on bereavement leave, I received a telegram ordering me to report to an army hospital in Coral Gables, Florida. This was the first of a series of moves from hospital to hospital, from here to there, and then home. Along the way, my health problem was finally diagnosed as asthma.

My final duty station was Camp Patrick Henry near Newport News, Virginia. While stationed there, I still had enough free time to take care of some personal things. An opportunity fell into my lap when I saw a notice posted on the bulletin board announcing classes for soldiers to learn to weld and become certified welders. I knew that welders were always in demand in San Diego, and I wanted to take the courses, but I was afraid to ask permission because of my asthma. I decided it would be easier to apologize than to ask permission, so I simply signed up and learned a new skill. I am a certified welder. I never practiced it much, but it came in handy when I needed a job the most. Today, if anybody needs a shaky eighty-six-year-old welder, I am ready.

While I was at Camp Patrick Henry, I made new friends, men I would never have met in the barrio. Soldiers called Nisei who were in the 442nd Regimental Combat Team from Hawaii were passing through on the way to Europe, and I became friends with several of them. The 442nd Regimental Combat Team was an outfit that at full strength would number 4,500 men. They earned 3,900 individual decorations. The following is a paragraph from a Web site devoted to the 442nd.

> The average height was about 5'4", average weight about 125 pounds, they had almond eyes and brown skin, and liked rice. They had funny sounding names like Kazumura, Hirata, and Inouye. But they played baseball, listened to big band music, and were Americans . . . almost. They were for the most part second generation Japanese-Americans and their country was just attacked by the Empire of Japan.
>
> —http://www.katonk.com/442nd/442/page1.html

I, a 5'4", 140-pound Hispanic so dark they called me Shadow, felt a kinship with those guys. Like them I was an American . . . almost. Some years later I had an opportunity to chat with one of them, Senator Daniel Inouye of Hawaii. What a great man he was! Inouye had enlisted as a private, became a captain, earned the Medal of Honor, and lost an arm in Italy. Yet, after he returned to the United States, this great American suffered the pangs of prejudice. The following is a clip from a 2000 article in the *Nichi Bei Times Online*.

> A barber in a small town outside of San Francisco in 1945 refused to give a haircut to Captain Inouye, whose chest was decorated with several honors, and whose empty right sleeve gave vivid testimony of what was sacrificed for his country. "We don't serve Japs here," the barber told Inouye.
> —http://www.javoice.com/nichi_bei.html

Our proud nation helped promote freedom and equality throughout the world, but the perception of too many Americans is that our heroes have to be tall white men. I've always tried to change that perception and always will. America will not have completed her promise to the huddled masses until it does.

On August 18, 1944, my army service ended when I was given a medical discharge because of asthma. I would be able to pursue my dream of being a college graduate. The same nation that discriminated against people of color made it possible for many of them to get a coveted college degree. I was one of many thousands of returning veterans who went to college on the GI Bill.

My tween years were over. They had been exciting ones.

CHAPTER FOUR

The Girl from
Across the Street, 1944–45

By late August of 1944, I was back in Barrio Logan. The war was raging in both hemispheres, but the result was no longer in doubt. We were going to win. My country and its allies had pulled off the world's biggest and riskiest invasion on the beaches of Normandy. Our armies, firmly entrenched in northern Europe, were slogging toward a certain, if costly, victory. In the Far East, we were advancing, island by island, toward another sure and equally costly victory. Ahead lay tremendous battles in Belgium and Okinawa, and places hitherto unknown, such as Iwo Jima, but the Allies were not going to be stopped.

The United States had a terrible weapon in the works. Two years earlier, scientists at the University of Chicago had produced the world's first self-sustaining nuclear chain reaction in a nuclear pile. This would lead to the development of the atom bomb that ended the last war to end all wars.

On our way to defeating two of the most despotic regimes in the history of the world, we had opened either Pandora's box or the door to a technological explosion, the likes of which the world had never seen. The answer is still out on that question.

During my time in the army, I had changed. I was now a citizen and an eligible voter. I was much more mature than when I had boarded that bus to San Pedro in December of 1942. My stint in the army gave me an understanding of the world I'd never had before. I had seen parts of my country and the world that were as alien to me as another planet. I had traveled to the only country in the hemisphere where neither of the languages I spoke was the official language. I lived with folks who had never met a person of Mexican descent. Upon my return, I was a changed man. I was ready to take my place as an adult in this burgeoning country I had sworn to defend.

I wanted to be ready. I would get the higher education that my parents wanted me to get and I'd always dreamt of. But more importantly, I would marry the girl who would be with me for the rest of my life.

This story is slightly out of sequence, but I am including it here because important events tend to overlap, and our marriage won't fit into a nice, neat time frame. Also, it was the happiest event of my life, and I am, as my Anglo friends might say, busting my britches to tell it.

I didn't exactly discover the woman who would be my wife. After all, she was born across the street from me when I was almost ten years old. To me, Beatriz Serrano was always just a kid, and a girl at that! What guy in the barrio really gave a hoot about little girls, even if the grown-ups thought they were cute? Beatriz was there, but who cared?

But that was before she grew up.

As I have mentioned before, Our Lady of Guadalupe and the Catholic Youth Organization (CYO) were pretty much the center of social life for Latino youngsters in my neighborhood. I'd played baseball on CYO teams and attended chaperoned dances held by the organization. Although I wasn't always so keen on the chaperones, the dances proved to be a sensible way to introduce kids to adult life. Indeed, chaperoned or not, the CYO dances were a highlight of my youth well into my twenties.

One night a few years after my army discharge, I saw a young beauty at a CYO dance. Could she dance! She was so graceful and light on her feet. I was a bit leery of even asking her out onto the floor—she was much better than I, and she was that little girl from across the street.

My goodness! When I was in high school, she was just a skinny little kid with curly black hair, of little interest to a macho dude like me.

But she wasn't a little girl anymore. Beatriz Serrano was now sixteen, a young adult. She and her sister Consuelo had been accomplished dancers and singers for most of their lives, starting about the time I was a sophomore in high school. They even took lessons at the Radcliff House on Broadway, which led to some special appearances at one of San Diego's infamous places of entertainment, the

Hollywood Burlesque House. Of course, they never shared the stage with San Diego's infamous Spiderwoman or with Gypsy Rose Lee.

Usually Consuelo would play the male in one of the traditional Mexican dances, and would even wear a fake mustache. Beatriz would play the girl. These were the sort of dances where the girl would wear sequined skirts and fancy headdresses.

Looking back, I'm not sure how much of this I knew when I saw the beauty, one inch shy of five feet tall, at the CYO hall and wanted to dance with her, but this was as daunting as any challenge I would receive from the likes of my old wrestling coach Frank Crosby. I had enough sense to realize I was outclassed on the dance floor.

I had to impress this young woman that I towered over by five inches and outweighed by fifty pounds. If dancing had been wrestling, I'd have been an easy favorite, but it wasn't. It was dancing, and I was outclassed. I was as scared of her as I would have been if a sumo wrestler had stepped into the ring against me.

I took lessons at the Neighborhood House to close the gap.

Thus prepared, one night I finally approached the girl I had once held in contempt because she was just a kid, and I asked her to dance. I later learned she had been wondering what that cute GI just out of the army was waiting on.

It went well. I wasn't on Beatriz's level (and still am not), but I was certainly better than most of the other guys at the CYO hall. After all, I had taken lessons and had enough coordination to be a wrestling champion, as well as a boxer who had lost only one bout. Dancing just wasn't a big mystery. Soon we became *the* couple on the floor. Too late for the Charleston, too early for the cha cha cha, and far too modest for lap dancing, Bea and I did everything else—traditional Mexican dances, jitterbug, waltzes, and slow two-step tunes. When I made a mistake, she was able to cover it up immediately.

I thought she was poetry in motion, but I may have been biased. I was falling in love with that little girl from across the street. And it was more than just the passion of love. I just plain liked being wherever she was.

She was my girl, and I was her guy. After a while, a short while in fact, I asked her if she would marry me after I graduated from college and she from high school.

She said the magic word, "yes."

Although both of us were Americans, our parents hailed from Mexico, and they were traditional. We wanted to honor those traditions, so we decided to do things the old-fashioned way, by getting formal permission. I started with my dad. He was surprised but pleased with my choice and the fact that I was adhering to the old custom.

He called Bea's parents, Simon and Esperanza, and made an appointment with them. On the appointed night, two nervous Rodriguez fellows knocked on their door. We were greeted cordially by two nervous Serranos—three counting Beatriz. Still, all went well, or so we thought. Despite the usual misgivings, we all agreed that we would be married as we had planned—right after our graduations, about a year down the road.

It was settled. She went from just being my girl to being the girl I would marry. Then, there was trouble. I committed the error of arguing with a priest on the priest's own turf, the CYO hall. I challenged him on some long-forgotten and, I'm sure, unimportant subject. We went at it pretty good. Then I forgot about it, figuring it was all over.

But I was wrong. I must have hit a nerve, because the priest called Bea's mother and told her I was the wrong man for her daughter. That was devastating. We were in love, and we saw our future ahead. Even if we waited another year until we both graduated from school, we still wouldn't have the blessings of either our church or Bea's family.

A couple days after the bad news, Bea gave me a call from the women's club where she was attending a concert. She had been crying, but she insisted that she wanted to be my wife no matter what the priest or her parents said. We had a long, soul-searching talk and came to a decision.

Like my own mom and dad nearly fifty years earlier, we would skip the religious ceremony and marry in a civil one. But even that wouldn't be possible in California. Bea was seventeen, and she would need her parents' permission. And they had already agreed with the priest that I wasn't to be their son-in-law.

Fortunately, Arizona's laws were more accommodating to young lovers. We talked my good friend José Ramirez into taking us 150 miles across the desert to Yuma, Arizona, where we found a justice of the peace. José was our witness while the bored judge mumbled some words, and Beatriz Serrano became Beatriz Rodriguez.

That was that! But was it? Was the marriage really valid in California? We were afraid it wasn't. What if her dad had me arrested for marrying an underage girl? And what about the church we both were raised in? We didn't really want to turn our backs on it.

It was a long trip back to San Diego. When we got there, we had my friend and chauffeur take on an even more difficult task than driving a couple of lovebirds back and forth some 150 miles across the desert on a lonely two-lane highway. José Ramirez was elected to tell Simon and Esperanza Serrano that they had a new addition to their family.

Fortunately, José was a good choice as an intermediary. He had been a combat fighter-pilot and an officer. Responsibilities like that give a person the self-confidence and maturity to take on difficult tasks. And he did have a difficult task. This young man, about my age, had to convince a couple of traditionalists with strong ties to Mexico and the church to see things through the eyes of their daughter, not to mention their brand new son-in-law.

I'm sure Esperanza was the hardest to convince. Simon was a big husky guy who had worked as a laborer all his life, but his wife seemed to be the more insistent about having things done in what she considered the proper way.

Whatever diplomacy José used, it worked. A situation fraught with danger to not just two young lovers, but to two entire families, was on the way to being defused. Bea's parents asked to see us, and we cautiously went over to their house.

Clearly, a compromise was in order, and compromise we did. Everybody gave in a bit. The offended priest stopped his interference and kept his peace. Bea's parents agreed that we should be married now and not a year down the road. Bea went home to plan an official Catholic wedding, and I breathed a big sigh of relief. I would indeed marry the woman I'd fallen in love with.

The wedding would have been anticlimactic if it hadn't been so hectic. The parson at Our Lady of Guadalupe agreed to hold the wedding in a mere two weeks. In those two weeks, we had to have dresses made for Beatriz and her entourage, print and mail invitations to about eighty people, and arrange for a photographer and a reception.

FIGURE 6. Armando and Beatriz on their wedding day, 1948.

It made the trip to the justice of the peace in Yuma seem easy.

On Sunday July 18, 1948, we stood in front of a priest at the church that had been the center of so much of our lives and were married. (The priest wasn't the one who had snitched on me.)

Our honeymoon lasted a very brief two days, but we were young and in love. Surely longer and more expensive trips lay ahead. We borrowed Bea's parents' car, a 1941 Ford, and went all the way to Los Angeles! We saw the Grauman's Chinese Theatre and everything! That was about as far as my money stretched. When we came back home, there was so much to do. We had to find a place to live. I had to get a job good enough to keep two people going, and I had to finish college.

Old Tio Mando thinks he got really lucky when he asked that girl to dance back in 1947. We needed luck. We had to hold together a marriage that started out so shaky it couldn't possibly survive. That was fifty-nine years, two kids, four grandchildren, one great grandchild, and eleven homes ago.

We're still waiting for our luck to run out. Meanwhile, Tia Bea and I are just enjoying our good luck.

CHAPTER FIVE

A Civilian Again, 1945

After I was discharged from the army, I wore a uniform home, but it was different from the one I'd worn earlier. This khaki uniform sported the World War II Honorable Service Lapel Pin, but that title was too long for the pin and too grandiose. Typical of the generation of soldiers who came up with *SNAFU*, *Gremlins*, *hurry up and wait*, and *Kilroy was here*, some GI somewhere dubbed the pin the Ruptured Duck.

That was part of my world of 1945. As for me, I was out of the army and heading into the next phase of my life. (I wouldn't be married until a few years later.) But what direction would my life take from now on? My asthma had interfered with my military duties so much that the army gave me a discharge. How would it affect my civilian life?

Would being handicapped by a chronic illness allow me to realize my dreams? What about that college degree that I was counting on to help me break free of the barrio and confront the feeling that I, like the Nisei, was only "almost" an American? And what about athletics? I'd always been involved in competitive sports. Would I have to settle for the role of being a spectator the rest of my life?

Fortunately, the United States has long had programs to take care of returning veterans, albeit with room for improvement. Back in 1636, when the Pilgrims were at war with the Pequot Indians, the Pilgrims passed a law that stated that the colony would support disabled soldiers.

In 1944 I visited the local office of the Department of Veterans Affairs and got lucky. No qualified staff doctor was attached to the local office, so I was referred to Dr. Milton Millman, a specialist in asthma and allergies. The doctor spent an entire year running tests to determine what was causing my illness. I was poked, prodded, tested, and examined. It turned out that several things had caused my problem, and all were things that had been part and parcel of my everyday life.

I would have to make some changes. First, of course, I stopped smoking cigarettes. Pillows and anything else stuffed with feathers were out. So were egg whites and chocolate. And so was beer that contained hops. That meant that, not long after finally reaching the legal limit for drinking alcohol, my main drink of choice was verboten, or in my case, *prohibitivo*.

I had to avoid dusty and smoky places. As a nonsmoker, I was practically alone. As in virtually all American families of the forties, several of my relatives smoked. I tried going outside to avoid the fumes, but I couldn't avoid members of my own family. I tried wearing a mask, but the fumes didn't respect a thin piece of cloth. Finally, folks in our house stopped smoking while I was around.

That would be the first thing done today, but in the 1940s it was indeed a big deal. Smoking, even more than baseball, was our national pastime. Ronald Reagan advertised Chesterfields. So did Joe Louis.

But asthma was holding me back from the things I wanted to do, and an active life was more important than looking cool like a movie star or heavyweight champion. It took a big effort, but I kicked the cigarette habit.

Cigars were another story. It took more than asthma to get me off them. I kept smoking the things for years. Then one day in 1973, I was driving down a freeway in Los Angeles, with windows open and a stogie in my mouth. Suddenly a passing vehicle sent a gust of air through the car. An ember blew off my cigar and burned a hole in the brand new suit that Bea had bought me. With Bea's not-so-subtle urging, cigars joined cigarettes on the prohibitivo list.

With the end of my smoking and with Dr. Millman's help, my life returned to normal. I took medication, including shots, and it worked. Eventually I again competed in wrestling, even at the college level. I also played college football, but it was expensive—literally. I had been classed as 30 percent disabled because of my asthma. But when the Veterans Administration learned I was playing football, they cut my pension to 10 percent, which meant I lost two-thirds of the money

I had been receiving. Costly, but it was worth it. They haven't printed enough money to replace my return to good health.

And I did return to good health. After a year, the Veterans Administration and Dr. Millman already had me on the road to recovery. I stayed under Dr. Millman's care for ten years, and eventually the two of us erased the last vestiges of my asthma. I haven't had any problems for the past forty years.

I'm thankful that the Department of Veterans Affairs was there to help me out. I try to remind folks that something isn't bad just because the government does it. Those Pilgrims started something back there in the seventeenth century, and I'm glad they did.

Asthma or not, when I took off my uniform in August 1944, I had to get a job. Fortunately, jobs were not hard to find in those war years. It helped that I'd taken the time at camp Patrick Henry to learn how to weld—welders were in short supply in San Diego. National Shipbuilding was hiring. I applied and went to work almost immediately. While other shipyards were turning out huge warships, National was busy building and repairing smaller craft, fishing boats and the like. Still, welding was welding, and I got a chance to use the skill I had picked up during my spare time.

A few weeks after I went to work at National, Jack Hoxie dropped by. Jack had been a close friend at San Diego High. He was also the fellow who helped me organize El Club Amigable. Now Jack was director of the Southeast San Diego Park and Recreation Department, and he had a job opening.

The playground director, Barney Davis, was being inducted into the army, and his slot would be open. I pointed out that I didn't meet the qualifications for that job. Jack replied that while the war was still going on, all sorts of rules had to be bent. I could apply for a similar job and then transfer into the director's job when the current director left.

That sounded good, but I already had a good-paying job at a trade I liked. Jack, as always, had the answer for that. Concrete Shipbuilding Company, a company owned by that great innovator Kaiser, was building unusual vessels: ships made out of concrete. The company applied technology that had been used periodically since the mid-1800s whenever raw materials were scarce. Now with just such a shortage during wartime, Kaiser was again making ships out of concrete.

Even concrete ships had a lot of steel, and I helped build them at night, from 11 p.m. until 5 a.m. I worked at the playground job from 2 p.m. until 9 p.m. Life was never so hectic, or so rewarding! I had more money than ever before. Surely now I would be able to attend college!

The playground job gave me important lessons in learning how to deal with people—people of all ages. These were lessons I'd use time and again in various jobs. It was a government job, so I was accountable to the taxpayers, or at least to my supervisor, who was accountable to the taxpayers.

That accountability meant bureaucracy and regimentation and I had to learn how to handle both. I'd also have other challenges—to learn how to settle the inevitable squabbles on the playground, and how to be fair while satisfying all squabblers as much as possible. Sure, the kids who played on the grounds were young, but they had parents and grandparents. I needed to resolve problems at my level.

I kept at my hectic, two-job schedule for about six months. Then I worked exclusively as the playground director, and that gave me the opportunity to get involved in community affairs. Community affairs inevitably led to politics. The direction my life would take was beginning to emerge.

By 1945 those thousands upon thousands of young men who had been taken from their homes to fight a war started coming home. First it was a trickle, then a stream. Then we dropped those two bombs in August, and the stream became a torrent.

The greatest war in the history of mankind was over.

The GIs, now veterans, had been summarily removed from their civilian lives. Now that the war was over, they were returning to a world that had changed while they were gone. But they themselves had changed even more. They had killed people and had survived the killing in return. The Ruptured Duck signified that a veteran had served, but as the saying went, "with it and a nickel you could get a cup of coffee."

Perhaps the Ruptured Duck provided no practical help, but it signified a bond with so many. All of us—black, brown, and white—had answered our country's call. We now had a kinship with each other. Despite that, there was still discrimination based on skin color.

Just as a new recruit needs basic training to fight a war, a new civilian needs help to readjust to a life that is so different from what he had only recently been trained to do. We were part of what Tom Brokaw would later call the greatest generation. I'm sure the newscaster was referring to the heroic deeds of our fighting men, but I would remind the reader that our service to our country didn't end on August 15, 1945. America was changing, and we were to have a tremendous part in the change.

The problem of becoming a civilian again is an age-old problem. Veterans who faced readjustment problems established the American Legion in 1919. I wanted to do the same for my brothers in the barrio. I wanted to establish a special American Legion post that would address the special needs of the Hispanic community of veterans.

I discussed my idea with an old friend and fellow veteran, Jack Ruiz. We decided we would be the ones to take action. But where would we go for advice? We decided that as members of a minority group, we would go to those whose minority status was indelibly etched upon their skins—the Negroes (which was the accepted term of the time).

We contacted Mr. Bolden, commander of the Dennis T. Williams American Legion Post. Mr. Bolden and other members helped us get our post started. We wanted folks to recognize that this post was aimed primarily at Hispanics, so we named it after a man who could not be mistaken for anything except a Hispanic. American Legion Post 624 was named the Rudolph M. Martinez Post.

And a proud name it was. Rudolph Martinez was well-known in our community. He had been a high school wrestling champion. Later he became a featherweight boxer of some note. Before the war started, Martinez joined the navy and was one of the first San Diegans who lost his life in World War II. He was killed during the attack on Pearl Harbor.

Surely he was someone San Diego could be proud of. I think we did a good job of honoring him. Returning vets joined as fast as they returned home. We provided not only camaraderie and social events, but also information about loans, health care assistance, GI Bill opportunities, and the like.

With our help, the fuzzy fog of bureaucracy was lifted a bit, and we had a place to go tell war stories, something every service person has done. In fact, I feel we emphasized the practical (loans, health care, etc.) and neglected the camaraderie to our own detriment. A VFW club opened nearby, and soon our members drifted away.

I'm not bitter about it at all. My intent was to provide the services, and the VFW did that and provided the camaraderie as well. I was not only working in the community, I was learning how to be successful at it.

I now knew where my future lay. I was good at teaching, organizing, supervising, and managing. This work had started with El Club Amigable and continued with the American Legion. I'd be doing it the rest of my life.

CHAPTER SIX

A College Man, 1946–49

My father always urged me to get an education. I'm grateful to him for that, but I also had other motivations to pursue an education: I lived in the barrio of southeast San Diego with nothing more than a high school diploma, and I had served in the army as a private. Few things could have been more convincing. I believed that the green grass on the other side of the fence would remain off limits to those without a sheepskin.

I don't remember if my old friend José Ramirez and I discussed our options in those terms or not, but things like this had to be on our minds as we talked about going to college.

Fortunately, the country we had just served was willing to help us out. One of the last acts of our wartime president Franklin Roosevelt was to sign into law the provisions of the GI Bill of Rights. I'm especially proud that my organization, the American Legion, provided much input that was incorporated into the law.

The bill was intended to help members of the armed forces adjust to civilian life after they were separated from the service, help those who could not afford a higher education to get one, and provide opportunities lost as a result of their active military duty.

Unlike so many well-meaning laws, the GI Bill exceeded its promises and helped stabilize an unstable nation as well. It helped avoid a couple of the huge problems that followed the First World War: the biggest depression in our history and the Veterans Bonus March on Washington in 1932. Best of all, the GI Bill enabled many Americans—especially minority citizens—who would never have dreamed of getting a college degree to do just that. In turn those graduates inspired succeeding generations to get their own educations.

José and I applied for the GI Bill and for admission to San Diego State College (now University). Both of us were quickly approved, and we became college men. I even became a jock. At the urging of my old San Diego High School coach, Bill Raaka, I tried out for the football team. The SDSC coach was a fellow who would later become a very famous San Diegan, Bob Breitbard. Perhaps, for once, being short gave me a bit of an edge. Both of us were referred to as being built like fire hydrants. I don't think I mentioned that to the coach at the time, though.

Not only did I make the team, but I played varsity as a running guard for about half the season. San Diego has a long history of football, but I bet you'll not find in its rosters many varsity linemen who weighed less than 150 pounds and stood a mere five feet four inches.

I'm proud of that distinction, of course, but it came at a price, figuratively and literally. First, the strenuous exercise on newly mown grass made my asthma act up. It was touch and go for quite a while with my wheezing and panting. Second (as I mentioned before), when the Veterans Administration found out that I was playing football on a college team, they cut my disability benefits.

At the end of the season, I went to Coach Breitbard and told him I wouldn't be back the following season. He was sympathetic because he'd seen my asthma attacks and understood the problems I had.

That didn't mean the end of college athletics, though. I had been a good high school wrestler, so I decided to wrestle for SDSC. I even got some unexpected help from the dean of men, Mr. Peterson, who was very interested in athletics, especially the wrestling program. Mr. Peterson offered me a job to be a student coach while I was a team wrestler.

Being a coach paid the magnificent sum of thirty bucks per month, a dollar an hour on average. Still, it was money, and it was 1947, when gasoline cost about twenty cents per gallon; bread, a dime a loaf; and coffee, a nickel a cup.

I took Mr. Peterson's challenge and coached for a year while I continued to compete as a wrestler. Then I stopped competing to concentrate on coaching. Athletics were important to me—and still are—but my most important mission at SDSC was getting an education. Athletics only last as long as one's athletic ability holds out; the benefits of education will last a lifetime. I had to get an education,

FIGURE 7. Championship wrestling team,
San Diego State College, 1947.

and it wasn't going to be easy. I'd been away from high school for a few years, and I had been merely an average student in the first place. Now I was rusty.

Upon the advice of my counselor, a gentleman named Pfaff, I took not only a full load of college-level classes, but I also took remedial courses, mostly in English and math. The remedial courses usually took place before regular classes started. It wasn't unusual for me to brush up on commas, semicolons, antecedents, and subject-verb agreement in the morning, and then use that information in a freshman English class later the same day.

And thank heaven math is universal. I knew that the Pythagorean theorem held true for determining the height of a kite and navigating the universe. I don't fly a kite much anymore, but when I do, I don't worry about how high it is. But I do hope I remember how to do a square root if I ever head off to the far reaches of the galaxy.

One of my favorite subjects—eating—played a role in my college life, just as it had in junior high school, and my sister Catalina, now the more Americanized "Katie," was involved again. After Mom died, Katie did most of the cooking, and she was just about as good a cook as Mom had been. She usually packed leftover tacos or burritos. When I unwrapped the food, I'd draw a crowd, mostly Anglos. At least in college, I didn't sit under the table to eat. The college guys were more interested in tacos and burritos than the junior high kids had been. This led to a swapping session, a tradition that lasted three years. I wonder if peace, harmony, and understanding would be greatly enhanced by sharing food, especially if the cooking were done by one of the Rodriguez women. Perhaps we can get the United Nations to look into it.

College was mostly fun, but there were also unpleasant events. I was still the short guy called Shadow. I was still the guy with the accent. I still lived in a country where our heroes had to be white guys six feet tall. The social mores of our country helped maintain the status quo. College, perhaps unwittingly, also prepared us for the status quo. I look back on it as part of my education—an unpleasant, but integral, part.

Thus, when my old high school friend Bob Dowdy asked me to become a pledge to his fraternity, I begged off. I had enough problems just getting through school on a shoestring, without having to cope with one more rejection.

Still, Bob persisted, and I finally agreed to attend the rush party, and even took a girlfriend from the barrio. But I did not become the first Hispanic member of his fraternity. Once again, I was rejected.

Bob was upset, and he threatened to quit the fraternity. I urged him to stay, and if he felt strongly about it, to work from within to get the fraternity to change their rules. He did as I asked. He stayed, but he wasn't successful in changing the rules during his lifetime. His life was cut short. Bob was recalled to active duty as a bomber pilot for the Korean War. He died when his plane crashed into a mountain.

I have purposely withheld the name of Bob's fraternity. All fraternities at SDSC refused admission to Mexican Americans, so it would be unfair to name only one. Some years later, Bob's fraternity was one of the first to change its rules. I like to think that my friend's urging had something to do with it. Maybe it did. Things just don't happen in a vacuum.

With so many things going on in my life, coping with the challenges of getting a degree was a matter of establishing a routine that I could follow—and change, if necessary. I not only had to take my classes and participate in extracurricular activities, I had to work. Work was necessary to make ends meet, even though I had a big assist from the government. Somehow I managed to do all of it without throwing in the towel.

Fortunately, being a wrestling coach helped me make time for work because coaches were given some scheduling preference. I usually was able to leave my afternoons free as much as possible. That enabled me to land a good job as supervisor at the Neighborhood House, often referred to as a "settlement house." The job was one of the most rewarding of my life.

The Neighborhood House was on the corner of Beardsley Street and National Avenue, close to where I lived. The Marston department store firm sponsored the house, which was part of a system of houses established by an American heroine, Jane Addams. Addams started Chicago's famous Hull House back in 1899. It was set up to provide education, recreation, health benefits, counseling, and emergency housing—primarily to recent immigrants.

The supervisor job paid well for the time, ninety dollars a month for part-time work, but it was important to me for other reasons. It's been said that college doesn't educate, it teaches people how to get an education. Surely my education got a big boost at the Neighborhood House, thanks to two wonderful women.

The Neighborhood House helped in my education even before I entered college. While growing up in the barrio, I lived just a couple blocks away from it, and I got to know its director, "Mamma" Jones. Mamma was a no-nonsense director and a lady with a great heart. She, like most people in authority in those days, was white and Anglo-Saxon. I remember her as a "Mary Worth" type—gray haired, fifty-something, and rather chunky. She was boss and made sure everybody knew it, but she was also efficient and fair. Unlike many who held sway over others, Mamma never held her charges in contempt. She knew them and she respected them, and her charges respected her in return.

As recreation supervisor, I also worked with Gertrude Pieffer, a woman cut from the same mold as Mamma Jones. Gertrude integrated herself into the barrio and made sure that every dollar was well spent.

While I was recreation supervisor, my duties were much like those I had earlier for the Parks Department. I supervised dances, kept tabs on the playground, and ran programs for kids. During my senior year of college, my position was eliminated, but another like it opened in National City. I simply transferred a few miles south to National City and Casa de Salud (House of Health), where I even got an extra ten bucks a month.

And that wasn't all the work I did, especially after Bea and I were married. Like many newlyweds, we made do with very little of anything. After we were married, we lived with my sister Josefa a few days, and then we moved into what was intended to be a college bachelor pad. It had one large room plus a bathroom and a kitchenette. It was small, but it didn't really matter much. We were young, in love, and in the same fix as all the other veterans and their families.

In fact, the few months we lived there were fun months. This was especially true at the end of the month, when the checks from the Veterans Administration arrived. Then it was party time, mostly beer and war stories. Alas, bachelor-pad time didn't last long. After six months, we moved up. Bea's mom, Esperanza, bought a two-story house and converted it into three apartments. We took one.

It was about this time that I got my first car, a 1940 blue and gray Plymouth sedan with cardboard instead of glass in the rear side windows. This nifty car enabled me to take on two more jobs—cleaning the Associated Student Body offices and running the Loma Portal section of a shopping-newspaper route. I hired ten kids to deliver the shopping newspaper, a paper with a little news and a lot of advertising. With Bea's help, I arranged the schedules, got the kids on the way, and then checked up on them to make sure they indeed delivered the papers. I was a budding capitalist.

Every year that I was in college I continued my job as student wrestling coach. In 1948, my junior year, we made the Olympic trials and managed to place one guy, Rigo Rodriguez (no relation), as an alternate on the Olympic team.

The wrestling team kept improving. In 1949, my senior year, we knew we had a top-notch team and hoped for some first-place medals in the NCAA tournament. First, we'd have to get invited as an at-large team. Without any conference affiliation, we would have to be good, and we were.

Perhaps it was the lure of competing for a national championship that inspired us. I'd like to think my coaching had something to do with it. In any case, our record was just too good to be ignored. We won every regular-season match. We were in!

Then, as they say nowadays, it was crunch time. San Diego State was a relatively small school, and we were competing against some of the giants of the Midwest. Those guys just didn't lose very often to schools outside the middle of the country. We took a few seconds and thirds, and we never gave up. We may not have won any gold medals, but we broke new ground for our school. Until then, State had never sent a team to the finals. I was proud of them. It is one of my gold-medal memories of my college years.

So many of my wrestlers and fellow students went on to live successful lives. Three of them—Tom Pine, Bill Cowlings, and Ed Streicher—headed multinational corporations. That too is a gold-medal memory.

All the time I was in college, I was looking forward to the prize of a lifetime—my graduation—which was coming up in June 1949. I could see myself shifting the tassel on my cap from left to right while receiving the diploma I had sought for so long and had worked so hard for.

I graduated and earned my diploma, but it wasn't handed to me—it was mailed to me. A little six-and-one-half-pound angel named Ruth Christine Rodriguez interfered. My beautiful wife had a beautiful baby on June 5, 1949, just three days before commencement. Beatriz had needed me more than I needed the ceremony.

I certainly learned a lot more in college than they gave me credit for on the diploma. One of the most important things I learned was how to plan my life around the available time. Attending school on the GI Bill, part of the time as a married man, made it necessary, and I haven't forgotten the value of time.

I'm grateful for so many things, especially my dad and mom. Without formal education, they set a tremendous example by keeping a big family together through the Depression and by giving dignity to menial work. But they were painfully aware of the problems of being uneducated, so they insisted that we get schooling. For me, that meant a college degree, and with the help of the GI Bill and tremendous support from a wonderful wife, I got it done.

I left SDSC behind almost six decades ago, and the little school on the mesa is now SDSU, a full-fledged university. It is easily the largest college in the area and one of the better colleges in the country. Like SDSU, I did not stand still. I now have a master's degree and two honorary doctorates.

In 1979 SDSU honored me by naming me alumnus of the year. I'm especially proud that one of my students nominated me for the honor.

And I beat out a fellow named Art Linkletter.

For the past dozen years, I've been a member of the SDSU Ambassador's Committee. This prestigious-sounding group meets several times each year. We also send a contingent to Sacramento once a year to keep our legislators up-to-date on the accomplishments and needs of our university down here in San Diego.

I'll always be a proud Aztec.

CHAPTER SEVEN

A Teacher, an Administrator, and Almost a Politician, 1949–62

It's almost a ritual. Every June in colleges across the country, one speaker after the other warns the young, soon-to-be grads that they will now enter the real world. That means their carefree college days are behind them, and they'll finally have to earn a living. The speaker will imply that, thanks to the splendid education they have just received, they have the knowledge and the ingenuity to cope with the real world. For many, it is traumatic when they learn that they will now have to work.

My graduation wasn't anything of the sort. I didn't have to wait until I was twenty-eight to commence worrying about something as elementary as working. Working came naturally to a guy born seventh of eight in a family that never had more than enough money to stretch to next payday—if there was a payday. Nor did I first learn ingenuity in college. Remember, when I was a little kid I collected shards of ice at the ice plant and undersold the route icemen until they busted me. I admit that at the time I had a fuzzy concept of what's called fair business practice.

When I finished college, I was already working three jobs. I didn't need another job—I just needed one good one. That's what I had hoped college would do for me: let me drop a couple of jobs and still make a living.

Fortunately, this country will always need teachers—and I hope we won't ever forget it. I had wanted to be a teacher ever since my days as playground supervisor at Memorial Junior High. Working with young folks was a challenge, but one where I could see results.

Now I had my degree, and I immediately applied to the San Diego Unified School District. Within a few days, I got a call from the principal at Memorial Junior High, William J. Oakes.

Mr. Oakes was hardly a stranger. He was the principal when I was a student at Memorial, and he was still principal when I worked there as playground supervisor for the Parks Department. Now he not only wanted me to work for him, but he also made a special request to get me. He liked the way I had been able to get through to kids with special problems. And who has bigger problems than kids who have trouble learning? I would teach special education at Memorial, the school I was so familiar with.

Alas, a diploma wasn't enough to qualify me to be a full-time special-education teacher; that took a special certification. The school district accepted me on an emergency basis, not as a teacher working toward tenure. I would stay that way until I was officially qualified by the state. I spent every free bit of time studying, and I completed the course within a couple of months. But I wasn't certified by the state of California until my second year on the job.

Teaching special education was a challenging job. Even with my interest in it, plus a diploma and a certificate, I was unprepared. The special-ed kids needed a teacher with nearly unlimited understanding, patience, and knowledge. Studying to get the certificate gave me more insight. With that head start, I decided to apply that knowledge and get my master's degree.

I had my work cut out for me, but it was not insurmountable. To start with, I had my playground experience to help me. Then three teachers—Wilbur Hammersly, Fannie Paine, and Leroy Pharis—took me under their wings.

Wilbur Hammersly was my next-door neighbor both at home and at school; his homeroom adjoined mine. Fannie Paine was another teacher who helped me. She and Wilbur helped me over the rough spots. They were among the few who didn't consider special education to be a stigma. I'm so grateful to both. In fact, I still see Fannie from time to time. She is still one of the truly beautiful people in my life.

Wilbur's future wasn't so happy, nor did it last long. One day he was found dead in his swimming pool. We presume he was swimming alone when some accident befell him.

Leroy Pharis, another special-ed teacher, gave me inspiration. Watching him make arithmetic come alive for a kid was an education in itself.

I taught some fifteen kids from grades seven through nine. Each had a hard time keeping up with the class in at least one subject, sometimes in all. I had to help them grasp the fundamentals of reading, writing, speaking, and arithmetic. The rewards of such a job are wonderful for a person who is willing to look at students and help them become the best they can be. None of my special-ed kids became a college president or scientist or even a great orator or writer, but virtually all became productive citizens. That's a lot more than would have happened if they hadn't had someone who believed in them and took the time to help them believe in themselves.

My work as a junior high special-ed teacher involved five class periods that included a homeroom period and a preparation period. I'd certainly found *one* job that was enough to keep me busy. Yet, as always, I ended up with two. Throughout my stint as a teacher, I worked a couple nights a week teaching adults from my school district and the adjoining Sweetwater School District. I like to think that, thanks to me, some adults learned more about American history than they had previously known. I also helped some folks become bilingual by teaching Spanish.

As a special-ed teacher, I had an added assignment as home coordinator, usually carried out in the preparation period. This job required me to check on students who were habitually absent, tardy, or disruptive. It wasn't a fun job; each visit to a youngster's parents was a harrowing yet potentially rewarding experience. It helped build contacts with parents in the community, always an asset. That helped me educate the pupils. And educating students was the goal, my apprehensions notwithstanding.

It was far too easy to hang the label "incorrigible troublemaker" on a kid. Unfortunately, that is too often cited as the reason for folks to give up on helping kids. The result is that society is saddled with a troublemaker forever. Attendance and behavior problems require a lot of attention. Ignoring them simply costs too much for too many people. Memorial tried methods other than home visits to address the attendance and behavior problems.

Mr. Oakes, the principal, tried to help. He felt that part of the problem was caused by the long school days—days spent mostly sitting. He suggested we use the last period to get the students involved in an exercise program. I wasn't sure that I agreed with him, but I got the job of helping kids burn off energy. Of course that didn't bother me a bit. I have always loved exercise—still do, as a matter of fact.

I even had a room to use. My schoolhouse neighbor, Wilbur Hammersly, had moved on to become an assistant to the director of the district's guidance department. I appropriated his room and turned it into a venue to teach tumbling, gymnastics, and (guess what!) wrestling. As a former student coach who had taken his wrestling team to the NCAA championships, I knew pretty well where I was headed with this.

We got some mats and started with tumbling, then gymnastics, and then advanced tumbling. We became good enough to put on an exhibition for the entire school, with an unexpected result—kids who didn't need special education or special attention and often held themselves above such things wanted to join the group just for the fun of doing the exhibition. This was especially rewarding for my kids. Suddenly, rather than being the guys who were looked down on, they were the kids being admired.

I was proud of that success, and I guess it caught the eye of the principal too, because it led to another extracurricular task. The Optimist Clubs consider themselves friends of youth. It's an apt description because they did, and do, run effective programs for youngsters. At Memorial, a local Optimist Club had sponsored a wrestling club called the Trojans. The Trojans were successful even when competing against the regular junior high teams.

At that time, Memorial had a surplus of problem kids, so the Optimists started a second athletic club and called this group the Lions. I was put in charge of the Lions and had the Trojans in my sights. We closed the gap between us and the Trojans, but after about a year and a half, I moved. We didn't lose; we just ran out of time.

Wilbur Hammersly, who had helped me get established at Memorial, recommended me for a job as a visiting teacher with responsibilities much like a truant officer's. I moved up a bit on the masthead, and the paychecks were a little nicer. Being a visiting teacher wasn't much different from what I'd been doing as home coordinator, although it was more organized and more formal. No shooting from the hip on this one; it was now official business.

I was assigned eight schools in the neighborhood: two elementary, three junior high, and three high schools. My time was spent working with students and their parents. The aim of the visiting teachers was to help save kids who were in trouble. Few things can give one more satisfaction than getting children back into school, keeping them there, and turning a troubled young person into a productive citizen.

Education isn't all *readin', 'ritin', and 'rithmetic.* And I'm glad I never once ever used a hickory stick. That would have meant that both the student and I lost, an unacceptable alternative. But most of all, when you watch any kid reach back and use every bit of his ability and then achieve success, you realize all your work was worth it.

Jimmy Estrada was one such kid. He wasn't incorrigible or even what one might consider a bad kid, but he was delinquent now and then. That put him under my purview. During one of his absences, I found him and sent him back to school. Then I visited his parents. I knew from my fellow teachers at Memorial that Jimmy was a good kid with lots of potential.

Although we were years apart in age, Jimmy and I had a lot in common. I had been where he was now and could have easily gone over the edge when I was a youngster. There is no magic solution to any problem, nor was there to this one. I simply pointed out to Jimmy and his folks that occasional transgressions often become frequent transgressions. Then, too often, there is no turning back. Kids in Barrio Logan needed no help in going bad. I certainly didn't "save a kid" or anything like that. At the most, I was there when a kid needed some help. In any case, Jimmy completed high school and graduated from San Diego State. I'm proud of him.

I had no way of knowing that he'd return the favor many times over. In 1979 he recommended to the SDSU alumni association that I be honored as alumnus of the year, an honor I did receive. And, as I mentioned earlier, I beat out a fellow named Art Linkletter.

There were other students from Barrio Logan who were as successful as Jimmy. While doing research for this book, I had a long interview with Rachael Ortiz. Her office was filled with plaques, citations, and awards from mayors, council members, and nabobs of all sorts. She has touched so many lives.

The following is an excerpt, written in 2000, from the American Bar Association Web site.

> Rachel [*sic*] spent her own childhood in a children's home, in foster care, and finally in the juvenile justice system. She was born in 1941 in San Diego, California, then a very parochial, insular town—culturally and racially. It was, in many respects, not an easy place for a young Latina to grow up. But for Rachel [*sic*], a ward of the court until her eighteenth birthday, it was that much more difficult. She faced drug addiction, resulting incarceration, and everything that came with those experiences for a young woman of her culture at those times in that place.
>
> —http://www.abanet.org/irr/hr/falloo/schooley.html

Rachael survived all the problems she faced and then some. She repaid whatever debt she may have owed to society many times over, always working with the underdog. She worked with Cesar Chavez of the United Farm Workers and with immigrants in San Francisco. She helped implement a work furlough program at San Quentin, and was elected chairperson of the San Diego mayor's Council of Youth. Bobby Kennedy called her one of the most heroic figures of our time.

My interview with Rachael was held in her office in Barrio Station, the seat of a project she started in 1970; she is currently the executive director. Barrio Station, like almost everything else in her life, is aimed at saving the lives of young Hispanic kids.

She told me I had been one of her heroes when she was a kid in my old neighborhood, although I'd never met her "officially," that is, as a visiting teacher. "We felt honored to be busted by Mando. For the first time we could look at a person in authority who looked like us." She added that Latino kids knew they would get a fair shake from me.

I modestly agree with her, although I was far from heroic. My aim was simply to get kids back to school with help from their parents and as little fuss as possible. If I was successful, I would keep them from going through the court system. I never had to send one of the hundreds of kids I was directly involved with to a judge.

I was drawn irrevocably to special education, helping those who really could not help themselves. Special-ed classes had been instituted in the United States as early as 1894, in San Diego before 1926, then permanently in 1935, but that was about it. That wasn't much.

I had already decided to pursue a master's degree. Why not, I wondered, do some original research on the subject that interested me so much—the impact of special-ed programs. I reviewed a couple of studies and dug up other bits of information here and there. Then I started my thesis on special-ed students who were in the program in 1947 and 1948 and compared their success with students who were in special education in earlier years.

While I was teaching junior high students, I was also educating myself. Learning and teaching are both heady exercises. In fact, education—giving and receiving—should continue throughout one's entire life. It surely did for me. Like my students, I kept my nose in the books. During the fourth year after my college graduation, I was back at my old alma mater. This time I received a secondary administration credential, which, in addition to being the ticket to another promotion, added credits toward my master's degree. The education department of San Diego State accepted my thesis and awarded me a master's degree in special education in August 1953.

In June 1959, with a diploma, two certificates, and a master's degree in hand, I became the first Hispanic to hold an administrative position in the San Diego Unified School District when I was appointed vice-principal of Samuel Gompers Junior High School. Named after the early nineteenth-century labor leader, Gompers served the Paradise Hills and Encanto areas, or what is often called Old Southeast San Diego. Thousands of families of Mexican heritage lived in the neighborhood.

Jackie Robinson had broken the color line in major league baseball twelve years before a Hispanic did the same in the San Diego Unified School District. I had more than enough motivation to succeed. If I failed, I was sure the name *Rodriguez* wouldn't be remembered as the first vice-principal, but as an experiment that failed. Folks that would follow me who had names like Ramirez, Martinez, and Valenzuela would have to continue to settle for the status quo.

On opening day of school in September 1959, I assumed my duties as one of two brand new vice-principals. Jeannette Kramer, a former English teacher and a counselor at Lincoln High School, was the other.

I took a big breath and plunged right in, and it was some plunge. The outgoing principal, Jack Stone, PhD, had been an innovator, and teaching at Gompers was different from what I'd experienced as a student and teacher at Memorial.

Rather than following the style of most other junior high and high schools across the country, Gompers followed a team approach to teaching. Three teachers would teach the entire class three different subjects, one after the other. The time for each would be allocated according to the difficulty of the subject. With one primary teacher for each subject, the other two teachers were free to help by maintaining control and answering questions.

For example, the math teacher would be the prime teacher for the mathematics portion of a class that covered not only math, but English and social studies as well. During this portion, the two remaining teachers assisted the math teacher. Then the English teacher would take over. And so it went.

That was and, I believe, still is a solid method for teaching. It makes better use of teachers, and even gives them a better understanding of the whole picture. The students get more supervision and immediate help if they need it.

But the team approach needed a magician to fit together the parts. Teachers had to be compatible. Scheduling was a nightmare because it wasn't just three subjects. The whole gamut—English, math, social studies, art, shop, home economics, and science—had to be considered. And there were problems when a teacher couldn't grasp one of the subjects. Ninth-grade algebra is an example; it's surprising how few teachers grasp the concept of letters representing numbers. I hope that someday all adult Americans will understand that mathematical concept that was first used some three thousand years ago by the ancient Egyptians and Babylonians. Then, from that group, I hope we find some teachers who can make algebra interesting to kids.

Gompers Junior High was different, but it was always interesting. I loved it and thrived on the challenge. I was second in the pecking order, and after Jack Stone left early in my stay at Gompers, my immediate boss was the principal, Miles "Max" Miller. Miller was a strong leader who appreciated a total approach to education. I worked well with him.

But he left under pressure in my second year. Suddenly I was the principal, but I knew it was temporary. I didn't even move into the principal's office; I closed it and operated from my own office. Anything more would have been presumptuous and pretentious.

Miller was replaced by Robert Ford, a Stanford grad who was also a lawyer. Ford was a truly dedicated man who loved teaching. He never let you forget who was boss, but he was also easy to get along with. We all called him Bob. I got a kick out of comparing him to the Bob Ford who killed Jesse James.

Both Miller and Ford were good administrators, and I'm grateful for the experience of working for them. Every new job I had was an education in itself. Each gave new insight into education and the surrounding world.

I worked at Gompers for six years, until 1965. During that time Bea, my daughter Christy, and I also moved up, into a better home. It looked to be a simple move, just the three of us. We found an empty lot close to where we grew up and hired a contractor to build us a nice small house with two bedrooms, just what we needed. I had lived in some seventeen different places up to that time, and Bea had lived in about ten. We were set and happy. We thought we would live there forever. We would never have guessed that we'd move another ten times.

Within a year of moving into our new home, Bea became pregnant again—a surprise because her doctor had said that she couldn't have more children. But what the doctor said couldn't happen, happened. On April 14, 1953, Roderick Christopher weighed in at eight pounds and a couple ounces. We lost a bit of elbow room, but Roddy didn't mind a bit.

Things were going well. I was vice-principal, we were finally making a good living, and our family was one child more than we had thought we would have. A couple of friends, Mickie and Marlow Geiger, who lived in La Mesa, found a perfect house for us—with four bedrooms, no less. It had every amenity of suburban America.

The front lawn was nine-tenths of an acre filled with at least thirty trees—apricot, pomegranate, peach, fig, and apple. It looked like a small forest. Henry Wiggins, the art teacher at San Diego High, made a sign for the lawn/forest—Rod's Little Acre.

What more could we have wanted? Perhaps neighbors with a little more understanding of the country they lived in!

America is a diverse country and a land of opportunity, where a dark-skinned kid from Gomez Palacio could grow up to be a college graduate and hold a position of authority and of respect. But California was still a place where prejudice died hard. We learned some folks objected to a "Mexican" family moving into their neighborhood.

Thank heaven for an America that was changing. Just as some Anglos didn't want us among them, other Anglos in the neighborhood—including the Geigers—stood up for us. We moved in and kept a low profile for a little while. Soon we heard no more about "Mexicans in the neighborhood." Remember the slogan "Good neighbors come in all colors"? We tried to make that true for our neighbors. It surely was for us.

Soon we became an accepted part of the community and were involved in practically every community activity. Our kids went to local schools, and they were good ones. We were welcome in the neighborhood, and our neighbors were welcomed into our home.

Politics was becoming a part of my life. In 1960 I joined the effort to help elect Jack Kennedy. Although my main function was to get out the Latino vote, that wasn't my only role. Every election needs money, and I was asked to help raise it. Bea and I hosted a fundraising party, and our big draw was Jack's youngest brother, "Teddy" (Edward), who attended. The house was filled to the rafters, and people stood outside.

Teddy came through like a champ, especially when he decided to sing one of Mexico's hottest songs, "Jalisco." To accommodate the crowd, he went outside so everybody, including the neighbors, I suppose, could hear. Few things are as memorable as a Mexican tune sung by an Irish American with a New England accent.

Several people in the crowd remarked that Jack Kennedy wouldn't be the only member of the family to do well in politics. Indeed, he wasn't; he had two brothers who became influential politicians.

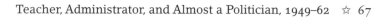

FIGURE 8. Governor Edmund "Pat" Brown and Armando while campaigning for John F. Kennedy, 1960.

FIGURE 9. Larry Montoya (president of the New Mexico Club in San Diego), Mary Montoya, Beatriz Rodriguez, Dennis Chavez (U.S. Senator from New Mexico), and Armando during campaign of 1960.

Also in 1960, I met Bobby Kennedy when he came to San Diego in an effort to get out the Mexican American vote. Bobby helped bring two big hitters, Cesar Chavez and Dolores Huerta, to town. Naturally a guy named Rodriguez who had started to establish himself politically came in handy in this quest for the Mexican American vote.

I learned a lot from both Kennedy brothers, and I'm sure they learned a lot from Chavez and Huerta. The four came from completely different backgrounds. The Kennedys were born and reared in a very wealthy family; Huerta was the daughter of a successful

FIGURE 10. President Harry Truman, (Unknown), Armando, and Hugo Fisher during the 1960 campaign.

hardworking businesswoman; Chavez suffered all the hard knocks of a kid in Arizona who faced discrimination that he fought against his entire life. Yet all became powerful players in politics. Perhaps *Democratic* is an apt title for my political party of choice.

It's hard to figure when I started to become a politico. I don't think it would be a stretch to suggest that my first venture into the field was while I was in high school and helped organize and run El Club Amigable. Later, as a veteran, I learned to reach across racial lines for help from African American leaders when I wanted to establish an American Legion Club to meet the needs of my Hispanic brethren.

My next venture into politics was with the Urban League. The Urban League, established in 1910, is the nation's oldest and largest community-based movement empowering black Americans to enter the economic and social mainstream.

Today it is almost exclusively an African American institution, but in 1950 the national group sent a representative to San Diego to establish a group there. As I had called on Mr. Bolden, a black man, to help me establish American Legion Post 624—the Rudolph M. Martinez Post—the Urban League asked me to help them establish a group in San Diego.

The strategy worked, and the local chapter was established within a year. I received a call from Mr. Percy Steele, who not only wanted to thank me, but also wanted me to serve on the board of directors. A year later, I was elected vice president, a position I held until President Carter called me to Washington as commissioner of the U.S. Equal Employment Opportunity Commission, whose policy prohibited me from serving in both capacities. My time on the board of directors had been an education as well as a political adventure.

Whether it had been my intent or not, I was becoming a political animal, and it didn't go unnoticed. A group of local activists wanted me to help a fellow run for the San Diego Unified School District school board; I was asked to be the campaign manager. This presented a couple of challenges: first, I was vice-principal at Gompers, which might have stretched the conflict of interest thing a bit; second, the would-be candidate was a black Presbyterian minister who hailed from Birmingham, Alabama, and we could get pummeled in the election because not a whole lot of black preachers from the Deep South held office in San Diego.

Still, as the first-ever Hispanic in any meaningful position of leadership in our school system, I couldn't turn down this challenge. I took a deep breath and dived right in. We were going to put the Reverend George Walker Smith on the school board in a conservative city.

This effort took a bit more than hoopla and bands and high-flown speeches. It also took a bit of subterfuge. Assuming that the blacks in the mixed district already knew Smith, I kept his face away from the rest of the voters as much as possible. I plastered his name, but not his face, on billboards. The major papers in town, the *Union* and the *Tribune*, didn't run his picture until a day before the election.

It worked. He won easily, and another politician was on his way. Smith eventually became president of the National School Boards Association. I'm especially pleased that he chose me to be a guest speaker when he was installed at the 1979 national conference.

All that political stuff and I never got paid a penny, but it was worth it to see a man like my friend have an impact on his community, a community that eventually extended across the country.

The entire community ought to have been pleased that Smith had prevailed and used his influence so wisely and well in San Diego. In 1970 he started a club intended mostly for his fellow African Americans. They would meet in a church basement, eat catfish, and discuss whatever issue was hot, or at least of major interest to them and their community. It was called the Colored Folks Club. Ere long, so many white folks showed up for both the catfish and the discussions that the name was changed to the Catfish Club. Today nary a serious politician would dare turn down an invitation to the club.

Another outfit with the same general goals, the City Club of San Diego, was founded about the same time. The City Club had a diverse membership, but was mostly a white club.

Today the City Club, headed by one of the whitest Democrats in town, and the Catfish Club, headed by one of the blackest Republicans in town, hold joint meetings. Democracy and the republic are very well served by two diverse groups in a community that is not yet as diverse as it ought to be.

In 1962 I got involved in a political campaign again—this time as a candidate. Beatriz got me involved when she was working for my sister Katie (Catalina). Katie was a politician herself, but not in the public sector. She was the business agent for the Congress of Industrial Organizations (CIO) for the local fish canneries, and you'll not find a union that's worth a damn that isn't political. The cannery union was worth a damn, and my sister had a lot to do with it.

Katie and I were always close. We walked to junior high together, ate under the table, and shared confidences. It was no surprise we both ended up kin in politics as well as family.

In the close race in 1960, I helped register Latinos to push Jack Kennedy in his race for the White House. I got to know Robert Kennedy quite well also. That year was also the first time I had the pleasure to work with two giants in Mexican American politics: Cesar Chavez and Dolores Huerta.

The Democrat in the Seventy-seventh Assembly District was Sheridan Hegland, who was leaving to run for U.S. Congress. Hegland had been a tremendous politician. He and Roger Reville were instrumental in bringing the world-class University of California, San Diego, to La Jolla. Hegland had been elected and reelected several times despite the Seventy-seventh Assembly District being predominantly Republican. I, a newcomer and a Democrat, would be a distinct underdog if I ran.

By now I was a political animal. Bea and I talked it over and decided I should enter the race, but it wasn't just a matter of running. As Tip O'Neill once said, "All politics is local." An unofficial but tacit rule in California said politicians had to be local; that is, they had to live in the district they represented. So first I had to move for my eighteenth time— this time to the Seventy-seventh Assembly District. A second consideration in my decision was that schoolteachers just didn't run for elected office, not in San Diego. So far as I could tell I would be the first.

Fortunately, we found a good house in Lemon Grove, safely within our district, and moved in. The kids loved it because it had a pool. That is, they loved it except on those days when they had to clean the pool.

After we moved, I began my campaign. The primary was easy, but the main bout was something else. I had to scratch for contributions, and that's a tough job unless you are the favorite, and I wasn't. My opponent, Richard Donovan, was a young attorney backed to the hilt by the Republicans who wanted to take back their "own" conservative district.

The Democrats were lucky to make it a close race, but we lost. Now I realize that I made a big mistake, one that, to me at least, had no special significance at the time. One of my mailers had a replica of the Mexican flag. To me the flag meant the same thing that a Hennessee or an O'Malley might say about being proud to be Irish, or a Hemmingsen might say about being Norwegian. I was simply acknowledging my heritage, not my loyalty. But a thing like that might have cost a few votes, and I had lost by just a few.

I'll always wonder "what if." But as an old saying has it, "Winning is like a fisherman who catches a lot of fish. Then he has to clean the

FIGURE 11. *Left to right*: Lionel Van Deerlin, Alfonzo Johnson, and Armando in 1962 when Van Deerlin won his congressional seat. He served from 1963 to 1981.

things." With the sure vision of hindsight, I could list a lot of things we did wrong, but the result was predictable, and I'm glad I did it.

I do remember some wonderful folks who went out of the way to help me. I can never repay Phillip Isenberg, my campaign manager. Phillip, at age twenty-one, was the president of the Young Democrats and worked pro bono as I had done so often. The young man later became mayor of Sacramento and an assemblyman.

My friend Lionel Van Deerlin ran for the House of Representatives. He and I often campaigned together. He and his son John "Pancho" Van Deerlin persuaded Henry B. Gonzales to come over from San Antonio and speak in my support. I made lifelong friends of both Van and Henry. Both were great Americans. Van went on to serve in the House of Representatives for eighteen years.

FIGURE 12. Armando with Henry B. Gonzalez, Congressman
from Texas, 1962.

Steve Gillis, an attorney and fund-raiser, worked hard in my campaign, digging into his own pockets at times to make ends meet. In the end, we paid all our bills and finished in the black.

My fellow teacher Dean Bistline worked with me throughout the campaign and even wrote speeches for me. We too became lifelong friends. Dean worked with me off and on throughout my career, and I just had a drink with him the other day. He is a few weeks younger than I and now lives in San Francisco. (Prior to publication of this book, Dean Bistline died.)

Running for the assembly was a learning experience, but it was much more. I made valuable friends whose paths crossed mine many times over the years. And I was now a bona fide political animal.

CHAPTER EIGHT

A Political Animal, 1962–66

Being a political animal is fine, except it doesn't pay well and often doesn't pay at all unless one is an officeholder or is on the staff of an officeholder. So I kept my job as a vice-principal while doing this or that for one politician or another, all of whom "would be extremely grateful" for my efforts.

Politics provided me a chance to make a positive impact on my adopted country, and I loved it! I had escaped the ghetto by becoming an educator and a political animal. Now I was making a difference in schools and in my community at large. Being a member of a minority is a mixed blessing. One is never without another challenge. Part of the reason I was able to make a difference is that I was able to reach other minorities and, most important, get them to vote. I'd done that when I got out the Hispanic vote for Jack Kennedy; when I helped a black man, George Walker Smith, get elected to the school board; and when I came close to upsetting a Republican in a Republican district.

As I became more involved in politics, my workload, but not my income, increased tremendously. I was involved with several volunteer jobs, and not all were perfunctory; one was an appointment to the California State Democratic Party Coordinating Committee.

My volunteer work kept my name in front of the movers and shakers of the Democratic Party. Thus I moved up a bit more, becoming a delegate in 1964. The Democrats were going to select a candidate for president—at least that was the claim. Actually, President Lyndon Johnson looked to be a shoo-in, as would be his slate of delegates. Nonetheless, the niceties of selecting those delegates were observed. Johnson selected Governor Edmund "Pat" Brown to choose the delegates, and Brown, having observed an up-and-coming newcomer, chose me.

In any case, just because the presidential candidate seemed predetermined didn't mean a convention wasn't worthwhile. Remember, this was politics. There was always a chance of an upset. It happened in 1940, when Wendell Willkie, a relatively unknown lawyer and utilities executive, upset the favorite, Tom Dewey, for the opportunity to get trounced by FDR. Even sitting presidents sometimes run into a snag. Harry Truman was almost passed over in 1948 despite being the incumbent. He persevered, won the nomination, and upset the heavily favored Dewey. Truman was another tough guy who never shied away from a challenge, or from hard work.

Even though LBJ was expected to be the candidate in 1964, there was still a convention to be held. America's political process feeds off the hoopla to get the campaign off to a running start—silly hats, inane songs, and all. I think it's a lot of nonsense, but like it or not, it *does* have a purpose—usually the hoopla gives the nominee a "bounce." Sometimes he bounces all the way to that house on Pennsylvania Avenue.

Although the selection of the Democratic presidential candidate was a done deal, the convention was meaningful, especially to Bea and me. We learned that the problems of Hispanics and blacks weren't all that different from the problems faced by immigrants from northern Europe and elsewhere. Slavs, Irish, Italians, and Jews—all were segregated and considered second-class citizens at one time or another.

My wife and I attended a number of national meetings aimed at Hispanic delegates. We got to know folks from all over the country, not just Mexican Americans. We exchanged ideas with folks who were from Puerto Rico, Cuba, the Dominican Republic, and other Central and South American countries.

We didn't all have the same problems, but American Hispanics had one thing in common—our accent set us apart from the general populace. The convention left me with a new appreciation of my country, its greatness, its problems, and its people across the land who understood things from the same perspective as mine.

I was grateful to participate in the convention. It was a wonderful experience, and it was immediately followed by another experience just as moving—Bea and I were going to go to New York, America's premier city. I had not been east, except for my stint as a soldier some twenty years earlier, and Bea had never been east at all.

We just couldn't be so close and miss out on visiting the biggest tourist attraction in the world. After all, we thought, we might never be back this way again. We eagerly took a break from politics and had a bite from what's now known as the Big Apple. The trip was a special treat for a couple of kids from the barrio. San Diego's Logan Avenue just couldn't compare with the Great White Way.

But New York City itself was overshadowed by that year's stellar attraction, the New York World's Fair. It was so grandiose that it needed two themes: Man's Achievements in an Expanding Universe, and A Millennium of Progress. The fair convinced me that if I were going to shape the future of my country, I'd have to know a lot more than how to reach Hispanic voters.

Computers dominated the exhibits. They were still relatively new, but every teacher and school administrator practically drooled at the computer's potential to revolutionize education. Still, I had no way of knowing how much they would affect every facet of our lives by the dawn of the twenty-first century. In 1964 the Internet didn't exist, let alone the "information highway" with its wealth of information just a click away.

Little did I know then that two decades later I'd be back in Gotham talking with a fellow named Dr. John Natoli about linking some San Francisco schools with Public School 33 in Manhattan. Nor did I realize that the big building at Eighth Avenue and Fifty-sixth Street, with the name Hearst on its front, would one day serve as an office for me.

When we returned to California, the election went as scheduled, and the political predictions came true, with Johnson winning the presidency. In 1948, when he carried the entire state of Texas in a primary senatorial election by only eighty-seven votes, Johnson was given the sardonic nickname "Landslide Lyndon." He earned that sobriquet in 1964 by crushing Barry Goldwater in a true landslide.

My job at Gompers was going well. I worked hard to get the parents involved in their kids' education, and I did it the old-fashioned way—by personal contact. The school invited parents to meetings twice a month, and most of them showed up.

Each teacher demonstrated a lesson and asked the parents to help make it work. The parents even selected kids who needed special help. The parents learned, we learned, and, most important, the kids learned. There's nothing like getting the folks most involved right into the learning process.

Along the way, Governor Brown appointed me to the Compensatory Education Commission. That required travel to meetings in Sacramento a few times a year. It was in Sacramento that I met Dr. Wilson Riles, a person I'd come to know a lot better down the road.

Bea and I were certainly doing well, and in many ways, life was just getting better. Back in 1961, our friends Mickie and Marlow Geiger had invited us to visit them in Estero (Estuary) Beach, some eighty miles south of the border. What a wonderful place to go to get away! We decided to return to my native land for at least a few weeks each summer. We set up a trailer, and we were able to escape for a few weeks of swimming, fishing, clamming, water skiing, and partying. Our neighbors were Mexicans, Mexican Americans, and Anglos of all sorts.

It was fun lolling about in my native country, but my real world lay north of the border. I had made big gains in politics and as an educator. But sometimes the two didn't mix very well. My record as vice-principal at a junior high was good, so good that Ralph Dailard, San Diego's superintendent of schools, had me tagged to be principal of a high school the following year, and not one in the barrio. I was given to understand that it would be one of the beach-area schools, probably Mission Bay or La Jolla.

Still, I had run for office while being a teacher. So far as I know, nobody had done that before. Many teachers were Democrats, but the guys higher on the masthead made the decisions, and they were mostly Republicans. By June of 1965, when the assignments of principals were made, I was not offered the job of principal at either Mission Bay or La Jolla. Instead I would take over the Wright Brothers High School, a continuation school in the barrio. A continuation school is one designed to pick up the kids who can't, for one reason or another, make it in a regular high school. Most often the problems of the kids are disciplinary.

Continuation school or not, tough job or not, I would still be a principal, and it would be my duty to ensure the kids were taught. I'd had plenty of experience with disadvantaged kids, including trouble-makers. When all was said and done, Bea and I were secure in the knowledge that I had made an upward career change. I became the first Hispanic principal in the San Diego Unified School District.

As it turned out, the job lasted just about a week. Around the first of August, while still at Estero Beach, I got a call from Sacramento, from Associate Superintendent of Public Instruction Wilson Riles. Riles was a black man, and a man with distinguished credentials. Born in a small sawmill camp in Alexandria, Louisiana, he had lost his mother when he was nine and his father when he was twelve. Before Riles died in 1999, he had been awarded eight honorary doctorates and many, many other awards. Today a campus building at Northern Arizona University in Flagstaff is named for him.

I can add only one more, tiny accolade—he may have been one of the most influential people in my life! Nobody gave me more backing than he did.

Riles wanted me to come work for him in Sacramento. I was honored, but I had to tell him I had a contract and had to honor it. But again I was reminded of the power and the pecking order of things in politics. Riles had already cleared the appointment with Superintendent Dailard and had his approval.

But I still had to deal directly with Dailard, and I did so by phone. The superintendent confirmed that he had indeed approved of the transfer, but he had a question, "Did you ask for this assignment because of your assignment to the Wright Brothers School?"

"No sir," I answered. "I was looking forward to being principal of a high school, and I would have given it everything I had. In fact, I knew nothing of the Sacramento job until Mr. Riles called me."

Superintendent Dailard seemed satisfied with my answer. He even suggested that, rather than resign, I simply take a leave of absence in case things didn't work out in the state capital. To this day, I'm glad we confronted the problem head on, and I'm sure both of us were satisfied. There was no lingering animosity.

But things were happening fast. This would be a big change from the world I had lived in since I started teaching at Memorial Junior High back in 1949, but, as always, Bea and I made a joint decision. We'd go for it.

As before, Bea was left holding the bag with two young kids. I rushed home, packed my clothes, and headed to Sacramento. Even my car seemed uncertain—it overheated. I scalded my hand removing the radiator cap to let off steam from the engine, if not from myself. This was an inauspicious beginning to a major career change.

Still, according to the old Bard, "all's well that ends well." My hand healed. My car recognized a nascent nabob and behaved. I started my first civilian job outside San Diego, and things were looking good.

I even liked the other two consultants hired along with me. One was Fred Gunsky, Riles's speechwriter and an extremely brilliant man. The other was Ted Neff who was, like me, assigned to the trenches in the battle for the minds of kids.

Neff and I were to travel around the state helping school districts with their problems, usually segregation problems. Some were real; some were a bit fanciful. With a subject as touchy as segregation, it's often hard to tell.

Our job was to intercede and fix things before the courts got involved. The courts could not simply cut through the chaff and get to the nub of a problem. We could cut a corner or two, and we tried to do so while a problem was still manageable. That, of course, sounds much easier than it was, but we were successful most of the time.

When I began this job, I was practically living out of a suitcase in a motel near my Sacramento office. Then I moved in with Ted Neff in his one-room trailer in the suburbs of the capital. Neff had set up his trailer in Davis, a college town about fifteen miles from Sacramento. Believe me, it was indeed a move up from a motel, and it was as welcome as a penthouse suite at the Ritz, all the more so because of our friendship.

That friendship was put to a stern test right off the bat. I, like the milkman, am an early riser. On my very first day living in the trailer, I, as usual, beat the roosters but not the milkman and quietly made my way outside to see the sun rise.

In a few minutes, my trailer-mate came out, gathered up the milk bottles, and turned to go back inside. I thought I should say something, so I offered, "Good morning." I didn't realize my voice was deep, perhaps gruff.

My friend was a strict Quaker and a guy without a good supply of cuss words for such an occasion. He could only gasp, "What the ... ?" Naturally there was a smashing accident. Milk bottles went a-flyin', and several broke.

I apologized, helped him clean up the mess, and learned a lesson: never startle a person carrying milk bottles in the dark, not even a placid, soft-spoken Quaker. Either that, or teach him words more appropriate to the occasion. I could have thought of some dandies in a couple of languages.

Changes kept happening, and I was lucky enough to be in the right place at the right time. The Federal Education Act initiated new programs. I continued working for Wilson Riles, but my duties were expanded. In addition to the new program, there were new rules and regulations. We had new staff members and had to train them.

It was a busy time, and I was enjoying every second of it except living in a one-bedroom trailer. Neff was a wonderful friend and a good roommate, but he wasn't Bea. I had to get my family to Davis before the next school year started. This wouldn't be without trauma for my daughter, Christy; she would have to change schools just before her senior year. We said good-bye to yet another house and left it rented to another schoolteacher.

Finally, we hooked a trailer to Bea's Jaguar and headed to Davis. Hey, things were going great. I had a good job, and we had even rented a nice place to live.

What more could a family ask for? Perhaps a family leader who had the sense to check the location of the Union Pacific railroad tracks. In the wee hours of our first night, even before the arrival of the milkman, an express out of Los Angeles came highballing down the tracks a few feet from our house! We were jolted back to reality, and we stayed jolted all night long.

It seemed like every fifteen minutes one more train would rumble past. Some were passenger trains whisking riders off to Chicago; others were interminably long freight trains heading to God knows where. It may be the stuff of songs, but the romance of railways was lost on the Rodriguez family.

So we quickly decided to move again. Fortunately, Americans are always on the move. When I was appointed to a great job in Sacramento, we left behind a wonderful house in Lemon Grove. A professor from the University of California, Davis, had much the same problem. When he had accepted a job in Louisiana, he left behind a house, and we were able to rent it.

Things settled down after our move—Christy adjusted to her new school, and the rest of us got the peace and quiet we needed. I went to work with a new title. I had come out at the top of a competitive exam, and I was now the chief of the Bureau of Intergroup Relations, a position I held for a year.

I had the authority to hire my own staff, and I knew the first one I'd hire: Dean Bistline. He and I had been friends since he helped me when I ran for the state assembly. He had been a teacher at Gompers, but left about the time I got there. Although we came from different backgrounds, we had a lot in common. We ended up good friends as well as political allies. He was one helluva speechwriter.

Things were going well but not perfectly. In 1965 David North of the White House staff called a meeting to discuss the educational needs of Hispanics in California. It was considered important enough that President Johnson's Health, Education, and Welfare secretary, Anthony J. Celebrezze, would attend. I was also asked to attend.

My job was to explain what special problems Hispanics had and how they could be solved. Surely I had a good insight into them because of my experience in barrio schools in San Diego.

I led the program off with a plea for federal funds and programs to help alleviate the problems we had, especially in the elementary schools. If such funds were sent to the state with the largest population, the government would set a precedent. But my job was clear— I was to outline our needs and propose a solution. That was my position, and I still believe it was the right one.

But not according to Secretary Celebrezze. Invoking the concept of states' rights and states' responsibilities, he tore into me and my presentation. I wondered how it could have been so bad. I'd certainly checked my facts and did what I had been asked. I felt my ideas were fair. He of course had a right, even an obligation, to attack them, but he didn't need to make it personal and racial.

Fortunately, many of my co-delegates—Anglos as well as Hispanics— rose to the occasion and defended me just as vigorously as I'd been attacked. The secretary went on the defensive and left earlier than he'd planned. Sadly, an important meeting fell far short of being the success it should have been.

Not long after that, Celebrezze left Johnson's cabinet. I worried that our tiff might have contributed to it. People disagree all the time, and I don't think they should back away if they feel their position is the right one. On the other hand, I did not want to be the cause of hurting someone's career. As it turned out, I figure I didn't hurt Mr. Celebrezze. He was appointed to a federal court bench by Lyndon Johnson and was replaced at HEW (Health, Education, and Welfare) by John Gardner, a Republican no less. I ended up working for Gardner, and I have the greatest respect for him.

Politics can be buggy, sometimes literally so. During one visit to Washington, a staff member of HEW arranged my lodging in a hotel. The next morning I was covered with bedbug bites. I was reminded again that while the ultimate power resides in Washington, we out here in the hustings have to keep our eyes on them, and we should be careful where we sleep.

There were bedbugs in Washington, but things were going well in Davis. The kids had adjusted rather well in their new school. Christy had the biggest adjustment because she'd gone from being a lovely young woman surrounded by friends to being the new kid in class. I had forgotten how difficult life can be for teenagers.

Meanwhile, things kept changing. Early in 1967, I started getting feelers from the White House about moving into a position in the Johnson administration. None sounded enticing until someone mentioned HEW. HEW's agenda was my bailiwick. Of course I was interested.

It was triggered by events starting some ten years earlier and whose repercussions continue today. I'm proud to have been part of it. Sometimes I'm amazed at the difference we've made in human rights. Other times I'm saddened by how far we have to go. All the time I realize we must keep trying.

CHAPTER NINE

Help from the Anglos

Terms like Mexican American, African American, and Nisei are often disparaged by those who say, "We're all Americans." That's true—or would be if the word *American* didn't apply to every citizen of this hemisphere. One of the great things about being an American is that we can hang on to our culture. We do it with our songs, our dress, and our food. I believe one of the biggest drawbacks of ethnic pride is that it might help those of a different ethnicity to exclude us. Then we exclude them, and so it goes.

I don't remember if I was thinking along those lines when I helped start El Club Amigable in high school. It was a club meant to support Latinos who were largely excluded from many of the social functions of San Diego High School in the 1930s. Still, I insisted that the "gobble gobble club," as it came to be known, was not to be exclusively for Latinos.

I know I wasn't thinking along the lines of racial diversity in school when I counted among my good friends a couple of brothers named Frank and Jimmy Keniston. I was also buddies with other guys with unusual names—unusual from the viewpoint of a Mexican American—like Jimmy Bollin, Don Arnold, John Dobson, Bob Dowdy, Dan Ballinger, Ed Barnes, and other northern European names. It wasn't deliberate; I just found guys I liked and hung out with them. I even contributed to cross-cultural understanding by swapping tamales for bologna sandwiches.

It isn't easy to ignore different skin tones, accents, and all the other trappings of ethnicity. I hope if I am ever remembered by historians, I will be remembered as a fighter for minority rights. On the other hand, I hope the writers of history don't simply assume that having the name *Rodriguez* means I concentrated on Hispanic problems exclusively. Many of the problems Hispanics faced were the same as those faced by earlier immigrants from northern Europe—or Anglos, as I prefer to call them. Their hurdles made ours more manageable. I first realized that while attending the Democratic National Convention in 1964.

Over my lifetime, I have been influenced by people who didn't resemble me in looks, color, or speech patterns. One was a fellow who also influenced an entire generation of twentieth-century workers: Saul Alinsky. This famous firebrand established the Chicago-based Industrial Areas Foundation, which sought to build a network of affiliates focused on specific social and political goals. According to Alinsky, its main goal was to build affiliates focused on power, and its chief product was social change. *Power*, more than any other word, described Alinsky. I have no idea of the etymology of "power to the people," the term so popular in the 1960s, but I bet somewhere that famous firebrand used it.

When I got involved in politics and took up social justice as a cause, it was inevitable that I meet Alinsky. It was another hell-raising champion of workers' rights that introduced us: Cesar Chavez. My involvement with Alinsky was brief, but one I could never forget. He is remembered today with equal parts admiration and loathing. Now, there's a man who made an impact!

Chavez introduced me to another guy with whom I became much more involved—Fred Ross, who, like Chavez, had been a farmworker. He was an uneducated man, but, oh, such a wise one. Even though I'm an educator, I have to admit that schooling isn't always necessary for wisdom.

That surely was true in Ross's case. He never forgot what stoop labor was like. Nor did he ever forget the people who still did stoop labor, or the trouble those people had. More than anybody I ever knew, Fred Ross was able to focus completely on the problem at hand.

Another Anglo who influenced me was Charlie Erickson, who looked about as much like a Latino as Abe Lincoln. Charlie was of Irish and Norse extraction, but was married to a beautiful woman from Oaxaca. From the time I first met him in the mid-fifties, he was involved with the problems of Mexican Americans and labor.

In fact, it was a labor issue that brought us together. While I was vice-principal of Gompers Junior High, I was asked to go to Los Angeles to arbitrate a labor dispute between Charlie's union and a similar one. Neither union had any representation in San Diego, so I was considered neutral.

Now, fifty years later, neither Charlie nor I remember the details—not even the name of Charlie's union. That's ironic because much of the squabble was over its naming rights. The union is now the Association of Mexican American Educators, and it has branches throughout America's Southwest. I think it's a very good union.

In 1966 I was working as a consultant in the Bureau of Intergroup Relations for the California State Department of Education, on loan from the San Diego Unified School District. Later that year I would replace Dr. Wilson Riles as the chief of the bureau when Dr. Riles became director of compensatory education.

THE ALBUQUERQUE WALKOUT

In 1966 I participated in a conference in Washington about the needs of Mexican Americans, an ethnic group of special interest to President Johnson. At the meetings, questions were raised about how the Equal Employment Opportunity Commission might affect the Spanish-speaking population: Would EEOC have staff who could communicate with these and other limited-English speakers? At what level? Was there going to be information about EEOC services directed to the Spanish-speaking and other limited-English-speaking populations? Where and how could these services be obtained? Would language be a problem? Would there be a Hispanic commissioner?

That fall a conference was called by Commissioner Franklin D. Roosevelt Jr., chairman of the EEOC. It would be held at the University of New Mexico in Albuquerque. The theme was how to improve EEOC services for Mexican Americans.

I arrived in Albuquerque a day before the conference was to start, and immediately learned that one of the things we needed most wasn't going to be there—a high-profile chairman. Roosevelt was not going to attend the conference. Instead, a brand new commissioner named Richard Graham would conduct the conference. Graham had no practical experience whatsoever!

The words stick in my throat, but I have to say we were *chingado* (more than just angry). I called a meeting of those present when it became clear that the EEOC meeting was not to be what was promised.

Distrust was rampant. What should we do? We had to take action and control the conference and the agenda. We had to show that the EEOC services were important to us. We had to have a commissioner on EEOC who was Hispanic. Then EEOC needed to address some of our biggest concerns, like eliminating "English only" in the work-place. Hispanic employment discrimination must be highlighted. Offices must be staffed to handle Spanish-speaking clients.

Those of us at the meeting started the ball rolling. Our ideas were to be shared with delegates who arrived later, even the next day. We spent the rest of the night preparing, and we decided we would walk out of the conference. We made arrangements for a place we could meet after the walkout.

There was almost unanimous agreement about the walkout. Even the handful who did not agree said they would support us and not show disunity at the meeting. I advised Commissioner Graham about what was going to happen and asked for his understanding.

The media mostly gave us a big yawn until Charlie Erickson returned the favor I'd done for him a few years earlier. He set a fire under things. First he wrote a press release. One writer for a syndicate was obviously uninterested; his only comment was that the term *Mexican American* should be *Spanish American*. None of Albuquerque's television stations bothered to send a crew out to report on the commission meeting. The wire services were absent.

That wouldn't do. We had an event of national importance going on in Albuquerque, and unless we got some good publicity, we would still be ignored. Charlie took care of that. He called one TV station and told the news director that he needed to talk to the reporter who had been out at the hotel. "Oh, we didn't send a crew out," was the response.

Charlie feigned ignorance. "I'm sorry. It must have been the other station. It was a good story, and it is getting better with a big walkout planned for today. Sorry." Then he called another station and repeated the story, but with the roles reversed. Soon everybody with a camera showed up, including members of the haughty print media. At the meeting, I asked to be recognized, and then I made the announcement that, because we were not getting a fair hearing, we going to boycott the meeting. I asked Commissioner Graham to carry our demands back to EEOC and to respond to them by action.

Then, thanks a bit to Charlie's coaching, all hell broke loose. Delegates were marching around, carrying signs, and shouting. We became the proverbial squeaking wheel to the administration.

Did it work? We think so. Not long after the walkout, five of our members were given a special invitation to the White House. Some time later a Hispanic, Vicente Ximenes, was named a commissioner. A few years later, another Hispanic, Ramon Telles, became a commissioner. It was no longer a revolutionary idea to have a Hispanic sitting in a position of authority where Hispanic problems were being settled. It was a practical idea, but it took a bunch of Hispanics and a light-complected Anglo to make it happen. I'm glad I was part of it. I'm also glad I escaped the episode with my skin. It could have had other repercussions. Lyndon Johnson became president by being a good fighter, some say a ruthless fighter, and I had confronted him. I fully expected to pay the price and spend the rest of my life as a teacher or educator.

Within the year, I was invited to another affair. Charlie and others had arranged a dinner at the Statler-Hilton in downtown Los Angeles to commemorate those of us who walked out of the meeting in Albuquerque. It might have been yet another first—nobody could recall any other time a group of mostly Mexican Americans had a banquet in that hitherto lily-white hotel.

Ana Ramirez, a teachers union member who had long been on the front lines standing up for our rights, went to Mexico and bought each of us a miniature huarache (Mexican sandal) with a note "I walked." I don't recall any particular new ground that was broken at the Los Angeles dinner, but it kept the momentum going, and we got more good press coverage.

Indeed, the whole thing turned out well, and I modestly say that we made history. We had to ruffle a few feathers to do it, but I'm sure Saul Alinsky would have approved. Perhaps one of America's consummate politicians did as well, because two years later, Lyndon

Johnson invited me to Washington to be director of the Commission on Spanish-Speaking Affairs.

Today, Mexican Americans hold high office, both appointed and elected, across the country. Things are still a long way from perfect. It is difficult to erase ingrained ideas and stubbornness, but we're making progress. I'd like to think that our protest in Albuquerque helped more Hispanics achieve positions of power.

Charlie Erickson and I remain good friends to this day. He started a mostly English-language news service—the Hispanic Link—devoted to Latino Americans and distributed through the *Los Angeles Times* syndicate. Charlie's syndicated news service is a highly respected source of information, used by media all across the country. It is now supplemented by the *Hispanic Link Weekly Report*, a national news-weekly that covers Hispanic issues and trends. I'm very fortunate to have worked with Charlie all these years.

Charlie recently told me that his two enterprises got off the ground thanks in large part to my efforts. I introduced him to several important Hispanic friends, and I also provided him with a huge mailing list. In an ironic twist, I was able to help an Anglo help us Latinos.

CHAPTER TEN

Working for Lyndon, 1968

In government work, nothing is more certain than change, and sure enough, just about the time we got really settled in Sacramento, things changed again. Those feelers about a job in Washington were real. In April 1967, I got another offer from David North at the White House. It was apparent that the president of the United States didn't hold a grudge, or perhaps he felt he needed another fighter in his administration.

This time he didn't want me to go to Los Angeles to argue with John Celebrezze. He wanted me to work for—and I'm sure he hoped not argue with—a guy named Lyndon Johnson. The administration needed a Hispanic in HEW, the Department of Health, Education, and Welfare. It was right up my alley, but although working this close to the seat of power was enticing, I had misgivings. President Johnson was a Southerner whom many suspected of still holding Southern prejudices against dark-skinned minorities.

Still, I had worked to get him elected as vice president and as president. And I remembered watching his plea to Congress to pass the Civil Rights Act. It was one of the most inspiring speeches I had ever heard, made even more poignant in a Texas drawl, an accent I seldom associated with someone who understood minorities. Now he wanted me to help him help my people and other people of color.

Change comes slowly and takes a lot of work. Prejudice was still rife in my country. I thought of the indignity that Hawaii Senator Daniel Inouye experienced when, even after receiving the Medal of Honor, he couldn't get a haircut in a "white man's" barbershop. How could I, a man called Shadow, refuse to try to correct the bias that caused such things? I didn't refuse, and I'm proud of my efforts.

Thus, in 1967, a mere year after I had brought Bea and the kids to Sacramento, I asked them to move again. This wasn't an easy decision. Christy, who had just completed a difficult year as a senior in a new high school, was slated to enter the University of California, San Diego. She would have to be left behind. Roddy would go along with us to Washington, but he would once again have to make new friends. I was commencing to understand the plight of friends who had stayed in the armed forces and moved every couple years.

Having Baby didn't help. Babies seldom do. This baby was a small dog we had adopted a few months earlier—at least she was a small dog when we got her. But things change fast for Saint Bernards, and the little pup grew and grew and grew. We ended up with a dog as big as a cruiserweight, 180 pounds, but she remained Baby forevermore, if only in name. We would have to find a way to take the dog along, and she would have to be shipped in a special cage. Then we would have to find a house large enough for a dog that was about the size of a Volkswagen Beetle.

Fortunately, Baby had been to college. The University of California, Davis, had a fine veterinary school. We had Baby checked out from snout to wagging tail, and then she was trained as much as she allowed herself to be. The one bad habit she kept was an affinity for martinis. Nobody could leave one unattended when Baby was around.

Healthy, trained, and usually sober, she moved in and stayed with the Rodriguez family for six years. When we returned to San Diego, Baby was so acclimated to official Washington, she stayed behind. I don't think she even said good-bye, but you can't always tell with dogs.

We moved to Virginia to commence my work with the Johnson administration and got off to a good start. I hooked up with one of my earliest childhood friends, Allison Henson, who was also my old high school wrestling teammate. Allison had made the army his career, and by now he sported the eagles of a full colonel. He was stationed at nearby Fort Belvoir.

Allison was married to his old high school sweetheart, Miss Edna. I don't know who hung the "miss" on her, but she carried it from high school, and it stuck. Allison and Miss Edna put us up until we could find a place to rent. Like I said, things can change rapidly in government work. Buying a house didn't seem like a good option, so we rented, at least until it looked like I would stick around. Later we bought a town house.

After we moved into our rental house, we went on a search for furniture. As always, my resourceful wife came through. Convinced that good furniture would always be good, she started searching the back country for her own bargains. She unearthed some pieces as old as fifty years, but still in good condition. With a lot of paint remover, sandpaper, wax, and good old-fashioned elbow grease, we restored some wonderful old furniture. We still have most of it. Some talented artisans made some great furniture along the Atlantic seaboard, and I'm lucky to have a wife who appreciates fine furniture, even if it is sometimes buried beneath several coats of paint.

I went to Washington to work, and I was paid well for my efforts. David North had insisted that I be hired as a GS-15 to give me the clout necessary to get things done. My new boss was John Gardner, who had only recently been selected by the president himself. Gardner was a Republican in a town then awash with Democrats, but as have so many dedicated Americans throughout our history, he demonstrated that dedication crosses party lines. He came to be known as the architect of the Great Society, a program generally criticized by many of his fellow Republicans.

Gardner was the man at the top of our chain of command, but my immediate boss was Commissioner Harold Howe. Howe pointed out that my job was to identify problems caused by heritage, language, and often, skin color, and then find the means of solving them. Nothing really happens without money, and for government projects, money and what it will buy are distributed throughout different departments. Mr. Howe suggested I meet with heads of major funding units in the Office of Education, tell them my needs, and elicit their help.

Looking back across many years, I am not exactly sure of the sequence of some of the events that took place early in my career in the nation's capital. I do know that for the first time in my life, it would be difficult to point to a job description and say that's exactly what I do. On the contrary, my job as a public servant was a mixed bag. It included ceremonial tasks as well as tasks that seldom fit neatly within a job description.

Although in 1968 I was a new and relatively small fish in the order of things, I was still among the highest-ranking Hispanics in the administration. Surely that was why I, a guy named Rodriguez who was born in Mexico, was among an American contingent invited to Mexico City in early October to help in the hoopla of opening the Olympic Games.

I was in the public eye, and the fact that I was at the Olympics was noteworthy. Having a Hispanic represent the United States was not lost on our neighbors to the south. Furthermore, I like to think my being there made it easier for Governor Bill Richardson of New Mexico, Mayor Antonio Villaraigosa of Los Angeles, U.S. Senator Robert Menendez, and countless other Hispanics to succeed in American politics.

Politics aside, it was a wonderful trip to Mexico City for Bea and me. We could have lived in a fancy hotel, but instead we took the opportunity to visit with a cousin, Alicia Parga, and her husband Manuel.

Part of the junket included an October 2 visit to a theater in Mexico City's counterpart to the Mall in Washington DC: the Plaza de Bellas Artes in Plaza Zoccolo. We and many other visiting dignitaries were treated to a potpourri of native folklore dancing.

And it was great! To this day Bea and I remember the ballet *Dance of the Antelopes* better than we do the things that went on in nearby La Plaza de las Tres Culturas at Tlatelolco, known in the United States as Tlatelolco Square.

But what went on at nearby Tlatelolco Square had a bigger impact on history than did the ballet of Mexican culture. I was reminded of this just recently when the Associated Press carried a story about how former Mexican president Luis Echeverría was placed under arrest for his part in a massacre of Mexican students in Tlatelolco Square on that same October 2.

Riots—or demonstrations, if you prefer—seldom take place on what would be called a slow news day. In fact, that's the point of demonstrations: to gain attention of the news media. Mexico was spending an enormous amount of money on the Olympics, and students, reportedly some fourteen thousand of them, demonstrated against the spending. Mexican soldiers opened fire on them, killing about three hundred people. Echeverría, then the Mexican interior secretary under President Gustavo Díaz Ordaz, was long suspected of ordering the troops to fire.

Our involvement in the demonstration was minor. When Bea and I left the theater, cops and soldiers were all over the place. We were herded between two phalanxes of cops and told to proceed directly to the waiting limousines. We didn't know what was going on, and I'm not even sure the cops and soldiers did, but we could hear what sounded like a hundred firecrackers going off. We scurried back to Alicia's house and didn't venture out the rest of the night.

Our involvement may have been minor; we are still not sure of Echeverría's. A few days after the announcement of his house arrest, the case was dropped because the statute of limitations had run out.

A couple years later, I was invited to a State Department dinner in honor of then President Echeverría. In fact, because of our common heritage, I sat with him. But I didn't mention the Tlatelolco Square incident.

With roots in one country and military and civil service in another, I look at things like shooting unarmed demonstrators with a sense of unease. For a long time, such action was considered characteristic of Third World nations. Perhaps that was so at one time, but we might just look at a couple of similar incidents in America two years later. Unarmed students were killed at Kent State University in Ohio and Jackson State University in Mississippi. A fellow who lived on the fringe of mainstream America, H. (for Hubert) Rap Brown remarked, "Violence is as American as apple pie."

I'm afraid he was right.

After returning to Washington from Mexico City, I was visited by two fellows from San Francisco, Bob Cruz and Rene Cardenas. These two gentlemen, both PhDs, were trying to start something named BABEL, an apt acronym for Bay Area Bilingual Education League. Cruz and Cardenas asked me to help them establish a bilingual consulting firm in the Bay Area.

This was exactly what the Office of Mexican Affairs was all about. Bilingual education would be the most important problem my office would tackle. As usual, after establishing that the need was there, the next priority, like it or not, was money. I got some government funding for BABEL. Cruz and Cardenas found some private money, and later I got a sizable grant from the Hearst Foundation. I'll write more about that later.

After helping breathe life into the project, my office kept in touch with BABEL. I was pleased to watch it grow and eventually become the National Hispanic University, a four-year school awarding both graduate and postgraduate degrees.

Early on, I came face-to-face with my first problem, and it was a political one. My original title was director of Mexican American Affairs. Mexican Americans certainly had problems, but thanks largely to my contacts at the 1964 Democratic convention, I felt the term should be more encompassing. The problems of Hispanics didn't stop with those of us who lived in the Southwest United States and had ties to Mexico.

I suggested to John Gardner that the title signify a broader range. Mr. Gardner had an appreciation for the situation; he was married to a woman from Costa Rica and was fluent in Spanish. He agreed with me, but he had his own obstacle, the president himself. The term *Mexican Americans* had greater political clout, especially for a Texan like LBJ. Gardner lobbied for the broader term, and I ended up being director of Spanish-Speaking Affairs, the only director in HEW.

As I noted earlier, part of my job as director was to find funding for our projects. Begging is never easy, even in the government, but a fellow whose flair for business included selling shards of ice and supplying half his class with tamales didn't see anything unmanageable about the task, even on a federal level. Diplomacy doesn't reside only in the Department of State.

But before we could spend money, we had to identify problems, and I had a head start on this. One of my tasks while I was with the California State Department of Education had been to do much the same thing. This time my efforts would be for the Office of Spanish-Speaking Affairs. The two would have some similarities. Hispanics are scattered across the country, and we needed to know what their problems were. Most of all, I had to learn how others handled them.

Knowledge gleaned from my trip on behalf of California helped in planning the trip for the federal government's Office of Spanish-Speaking Affairs. We had traveled to the obvious places, often for much the same reason. We traveled to Florida because, by this time, it had become home to thousands of expatriate Cubans. Of course, we also visited places like California, Texas, Puerto Rico, and New Mexico. But other groups of Hispanics with all their attendant problems are tucked away in other niches all around the country, so my team traveled to upper New York State, Connecticut, Boston, and other sites.

In California we had visited with those who had firsthand experience managing the problems we were going to deal with. They included schoolteachers and school administrators, as well as members of school boards, parent-teachers associations, the National Education Association, and the American Federation of Teachers. Now, as representatives of the federal government, we would visit many of the same places and talk with the same folks. But this time, we would have a national interest and try to provide national solutions.

Were the groups we visited special-interest groups with one particular aim in mind? Sure they were, but they were also interested in educating kids. I had to go where the answers were, then sort out real problems from what appeared to be problems but were the result of bias. I tried hard to do just that.

Before the nationwide trip began, I was inundated with bureaucratic issues and needed help. I wanted close comrades whom I could trust completely. One was at hand: Edna Henson, who had just helped Bea and me get a house. She knew everybody who was anybody in the nation's capital and influential people around the country. She gladly came on board, and soon everybody in the office was calling her by the same moniker I'd known her as, "Miss Edna." The name seemed so appropriate. She just looked like the wise aunt every family seems to have.

Before I left California, Dean Bistline had told me to give him a call if I ever needed help. I made that call, and, as always, he came through. Both Dean and Miss Edna were amazing. Dean was great at writing and organizing, and Miss Edna always came up with the appropriate way to handle something or somebody. One or the other of these fine folks had a hand in just about everything important we did.

Even before any fact-finding mission, there were interesting times. Dean recently called and reminded me of the air force general who he insisted was called Jack Armstrong. I don't recall the man's name or rank, and I wonder how I could forget someone with a name like that. *Jack Armstrong: The All-American Boy* was the title of a children's radio show of the 1930s and 40s. Frankly I'm not sure that the general had the same name as my hero, or that he was even a general, but Dean insists that was so. I learned to trust Dean years ago and won't dispute his aging memory now.

Armstrong (or somebody) had a problem at an air force base near Del Rio, Texas. He referred it to my office. I wasn't quite sure if this was something a GS-15 could handle, but it was my assignment. At least we would travel first-class. Jack Armstrong took us along in his plane, a well-appointed aircraft suitable for a general officer—maybe even an all-American boy.

The problem in Del Rio seemed to be that the local schools wanted to shuttle the Hispanic kids off to "their own" schools, but their parents wanted them to go to the schools closest to where they lived. Having no knowledge of the protocol for a problem that crossed lines I'd never encountered before, I invoked the name of the president of the United States. That would impress the military, the Hispanics, and those folks in south Texas not quite used to integration. Thanks largely to the power of Lyndon Johnson in his own territory, things got settled, pretty much to the satisfaction of everybody. Perhaps best of all, folks who looked different from mainstream Americans finally saw one of their own in a position of authority.

Back in Washington, as soon as the word got out about who we were and what we were doing, we started getting pleas for help, and offers of help, plus suggestions in every case. We considered all of them and selected those that fit our needs. Insofar as possible, we tried to solve the problems, or, at least, spotlight them so other means could be used to solve them.

But from a Washington perspective, we had to learn just what the problems were, and what national implications they had. To do this we had to go to the hustings and see for ourselves.

Thanks to Dean Bistline, Miss Edna, and dozens of volunteers who were anxious to see us succeed, we got the trip planned in what must have been record time. In four months, we were ready to implement our programs. It was now in the hands of the most important folks in Washington—the guys who held the purse strings. All we could do was present it as clearly as possible, answer questions, and hope for the best.

Fortunately we had a very important ally. Our project was part of the Great Society, and the Great Society was Lyndon Johnson's program. He was determined to see it enacted as part of his civil rights program. I had no idea how much clout one could have when working on behalf of a president's pet project.

In government, as well as anywhere else, one's effectiveness is determined in large part by whom one knows. One of my valuable friends was, of course, Charlie Erickson. About the time I came east, he did too—this time to work for the National Education Association. Although he didn't work for me, his knowledge of things Hispanic was invaluable to me in my duties with HEW.

Even before the trip, I was immersed in the duties of my job. I hadn't been in my new position very long before a couple of fellows, Raul Yzaguirre and his partner, Ricardo Bela, paid me a visit. Raul, a Texan, had hoped to start something called the Southwest Council of La Raza, and now he was trying to get it off the ground. It was an ambitious program that took aim at problems with education, assets, investments, civil rights, immigration, employment, economic status, and health. Up to this point, it had been a program aimed mostly at Hispanics in the southwestern part of our country.

La Raza wasn't a government program, so I couldn't be officially involved, but as Armando Rodriguez, longtime activist in things Hispanic, I surely could. Indeed, I'm certain that my leadership in the Albuquerque walkout had brought me to the attention of Yzaguirre. Dean Bistline and I made several trips to Albuquerque, Tucson, and Dallas to acknowledge La Raza, to head them in the right direction, and to help them gain allies.

Probably my biggest contribution was helping La Raza folks make good contact with the Ford Foundation. I made the suggestion. Later a representative of the foundation asked Charlie Erickson, "Do you think the Hispanics can make this thing work?" Perhaps goaded a bit by the implicit slur, Charlie replied, "You're goddamn right they can!" Thank God my friend understood people as well as problems.

Thanks to the recommendation of someone who was not Hispanic, one of the most effective Hispanic organizations got off the ground.

It would have made a much better story if I could have written that my word, unsupported by that of an Anglo, had carried the day, but we must look at the world as it is, not as it ought to be.

My officially unofficial participation wasn't unusual or even frowned on, except possibly by political opponents. As it was, LBJ's leadership helped spawn many similar outfits in this manner.

Today Dean and others credit me with being a godfather of the National Council of La Raza, an outfit that grew from a relatively small southwestern group in 1968 to one that now reaches four million Hispanics and has offices in Atlanta, Chicago, Los Angeles, Phoenix, Sacramento, San Antonio, New York City, and San Juan, Puerto Rico. I gladly take credit for helping get La Raza off the ground, but nobody should ever diminish Raul Yzaguirre's role in it. He nursed it along, expanded it, and made it work. He was president for thirty years. I recently received a press release announcing that Arizona State University had appointed Raul Yzaguirre Presidential Professor of Practice in Community Development and Civil Rights. ASU got themselves a good one!

While I was in Washington, I had to take care of my official duties representing the executive branch. The Office of Education asked me to meet with my counterparts in the legislative office. Guy Smith, a member of the legislative staff and a man I later worked with a lot, told me there was much talk on the Hill about bilingual education, and Congress members wanted to know what I knew about the problem.

I wasn't sure I had the answers, but I had experienced bilingual education firsthand as a seven-year-old kid, as a teacher, and as an administrator. I surely had a keen appreciation of the problems kids had when they couldn't understand their teachers.

The meeting went well, and I was invited to accompany Harold Howe—the commissioner of education and my immediate boss—when he met with a congressional committee studying bilingual education.

By 1967 bilingual education was a hot issue, and Congress did indeed pass a bill addressing issues critical to the problem, such as curriculum development, materials, and teacher training, but it was not funded. The next year, it was funded to the tune of eight million dollars. That would be a lot in any family's bank account, but it amounted to only four dollars per year per kid, and nothing would be left over for teacher preparation or curriculum development. We ended up with no trained teachers and no materials to use in the classroom.

My boss, Commissioner Howe, wouldn't give up on it, though. He called a high-level meeting to get ideas. I attended, almost as a junior member. With the others calling the shots, I did a lot of head nodding. Finally the consensus was that the Office of Education should get a foundation interested in funding the teacher training and curriculum development.

Dr. Leon Lessinger, assistant commissioner of education, had been a superintendent of schools in San Mateo, California. There he had worked with Randolph A. Hearst of the Hearst newspaper chain. Surely if anybody could fund a foundation, Mr. Hearst could. And if we got adequate funding, we could train teachers and develop curricula.

But who would approach Mr. Hearst? I, for one, had no idea. In fact, not having one, I was all ready to nod my head in agreement with any name, when I heard mine mentioned. All of a sudden, I realized why I was given the clout of a GS-15.

That seemed like a tremendous assignment. I would be required to ask one of the richest moguls of the information world for money. Rich people don't get rich by giving away money, but I had to try.

This job was much more daunting than trying to sell tamales in a Mexican American neighborhood. Still, I was being paid to tackle the tough jobs. I took on the assignment, and it happened to be one of the most fortuitous things that ever happened to the kid from Gomez Palacio, but you couldn't have told me that at the time. I'll cover more of that in the next chapter.

It was while I was working at HEW that Martin Luther King's Poor People's March of 1968 shook the conscience of America and inflamed the passions of many. The passions surely led to his assassination shortly thereafter.

A big part of the Poor People's March was for the demonstrators—or their leaders, at any rate—to meet with officials and present their problems and suggest their solutions. In turn, prominent people in and out of government made speeches. Today people remember the march as an affair of African Americans, but it represented the plight of poor people of color all across our country.

Following Martin Luther King's example, a Denver boxer named

Rodolfo "Corky" Gonzales organized a contingent of Hispanics. Because I was one of the more senior Hispanics in Washington, Corky thought I could be valuable to him, and he made sure I was.

First he invited me to lunch and outlined his plan. Then he had me join him on stage at a meeting with HEW officials, where he referred to me as their representative in Washington and asked me to follow up on the promises being made. I was flabbergasted, but I knew it was something I had to do. By and large, the promises made at that meeting were kept. I like to think I had a hand in it.

I also had a hand in the census one year. A major function of the census is to locate problems in our country, such as a need for increased services in education, employment, health, and social security. In the preceding ten years, the Spanish-speaking segment of the U.S. population had increased even faster than the population in general. The Census Bureau borrowed me from HEW to review the forms prepared by the bureau staff.

I noted again that—contrary to common belief—everything done by the government isn't loaded with inefficiency and waste. Much later I discovered part of the reason the project for the Census Bureau went well. My old friend José Ramirez, the same guy who had twice stood up for me when I married Bea, had earlier prepared the same documents for the California government.

Hey, we turned out some smart kids in Barrio Logan! And José Ramirez wasn't the only one. While in Washington, I became a doctor—at least an honorary one. Or maybe not.

I was held over from the Johnson administration to the Nixon regime. Nixon got lots of credit, and deservedly so, for establishing relations with China. As the world now knows, Nixon's efforts were dubbed Ping-Pong diplomacy, because inherent in all the efforts was a tour of China's table tennis teams. They toured the United States, beating all who dared face them. But the defeats at the table were countered by a closer understanding of our huge and potentially powerful adversary in Asia.

What isn't well-known is that other sports were involved as well as table tennis, or ping-pong as it is commonly called. Tiny John F. Kennedy College in Wahoo, Nebraska, had a top-notch women's basketball team. My staffer and good friend Dean Bistline knew the president of the school. Dean and I helped find some unallocated money in the State Department to send the team to China, much as the Chinese had sent their ping-pong tournament over here. By all accounts, the basketball tour was successful.

The following June, I was invited to Wahoo. There, in a sweltering auditorium, clad in cap and gown, I was given an honorary doctorate of letters. It was the first of two I would receive. Today there is a question of whether a small school that doesn't offer postgraduate degrees can proffer an honorary degree. Well, perhaps not, but I sat through one of the hottest days I can remember, and Dr. Ted Dillow presented me with a certificate that said, "The John F. Kennedy College of Wahoo, Nebraska, on the recommendation of the faculty and by virtue of the authority vested in them, the trustees have conferred on Armando Rodriguez the degree of Doctor of Letters."

I always thought I became Dr. Rodriguez, but I insisted my old friends continue calling me Mando.

CHAPTER ELEVEN

Travels with
Randolph Hearst, 1969–70

As I said before, people don't get rich (or stay rich) by giving away their money. Yet, in May 1968 I was assigned the task of asking one of the richest men in the country to do just that. I would go to San Francisco and ask Randolph A. Hearst, the last surviving son of William Randolph Hearst and principal heir to his huge newspaper fortune, to help a project the government itself had given a pittance to.

Asking for money was quite an assignment for the kid who had bumped along at or below the poverty line much of his life. Bumping or not, I had never asked for any sort of handout. I even worked three jobs at times. Now I was given the responsibility of asking for money to help the lot of others whose fortunes were equally shaky.

This was important, and I had to get it right. Prior to the meeting with Hearst, I did my homework very carefully. Nervous, I was looking for a way to postpone a difficult task. I called Mrs. Mehawk, Hearst's secretary, and asked how I should go about setting up a meeting. She informed me that an appointment had already been made by Dr. Lessinger. Mrs. Mehawk arranged for me to talk with one of Mr. Hearst's assistants, who gave me a quick rundown on what to expect. There was no backing out now. I couldn't even delay things.

I drove to the Hearst mansion, and it was indeed a huge mansion. Perhaps it didn't compare with the so-called Hearst Castle down the road at San Simeon, but it was huge by the standards of everybody except multimillionaires.

Now, with all the enthusiasm of a neophyte salesman making

a cold call, I drove out to the Hearst mansion and pushed the doorbell before I had time to chicken out. While waiting, I rehearsed the talk I assumed I'd give to the butler: "I am Armando Rodriguez from the Department of Health, Education, and Welfare, and I have an appointment to see Mr. Hearst."

But it wasn't the butler who answered the door. It swung open, and there was Randolph A. Hearst himself. He didn't appear nearly as nervous as I. All business, he gave me a quick introduction to his wife, and then led the way to the family room. Now it was up to me to make a case so dramatic that the famous newspaperman couldn't refuse to open his purse strings.

I knew my host didn't speak Spanish, so that's what I spoke—not a word of *his* native language for a few minutes. I could have been reciting "Jack and the Beanstalk" for all he knew.

When I saw his face turn red, I figured that was enough; the point had been made. I said, "I just spoke to you in Spanish, and you didn't understand a word I said. Right?"

I realize I had taken a terrible chance. He could have chalked my act up as a stunt and asked me to leave. Or he might have listened politely and uttered those polite words of dismissal, "I'll get back to you."

But I had taken what's called a calculated risk. A newspaper publisher knows how valuable it is to grab the reader's interest with a startling headline and a strong opening paragraph. I'm sure Mr. Hearst recognized my talk as the same sort of ploy. I had his complete interest, and I hoped he recognized that I was willing to take risks to make things happen.

I explained that his frustration was mirrored by thousands of Hispanic students across our nation every day, except that they have to endure it for not only a few minutes, but for several hours a day, five days a week when they are in school.

When my host admitted he hadn't realized the extent of the problem, I pointed out that few people who hadn't experienced it themselves realized the problem. But it was there, and it was a big problem.

Then I went for broke: "I'd like to take you on a trip around the country and let you see what I've been talking about. We would talk to students, parents, and community leaders. When we're done, I will ask your foundation to help us out, but I'd like you to see firsthand what needs to be done. If what I've said is true, I want you to help solve the problem."

I sat back and waited. Mr. Hearst thought about it for a while. Finally he said, "I will do that, but I cannot promise anything more than that I'll take the trip. If the trip convinces me, I will ask my foundation to fund the tour plus the other unfunded expenses until the federal government takes over."

Seldom is a battle won outright, and this one wasn't, but my meeting was much more successful than I had dared to hope. We agreed that it was too close to the end of the school year to go on a tour, so we would wait until October.

Nobody has ever seen a more relieved bureaucrat than Tio Mando when he walked out that door. Surely Mr. Hearst would not agree to take a tour if he wasn't open to the idea of funding the program. If I could now put together a successful tour, everything else would fall in place.

But I had not taken Murphy's Law into account. In August, Mrs. Mehawk called with bad news. Mr. Hearst was in the hospital for a serious operation, and there was no chance he could make the trip in October. My elation turned to gloom. I was sure that the illness would give my would-be benefactor a chance to simply let an annoying problem die.

But before long I learned that I had underestimated my persuasiveness or possibly the inherent desire of a man to do the right thing. In March of 1969, I got another call from Mrs. Mehawk. Her boss had recovered from his illness, and he was eager to make the tour! He even wanted the itinerary so he could start making plans.

Mr. Hearst was obviously serious about the whole project. I got hold of the folks who had made the original plan and set them to work revising it. This was great news indeed! I managed to get excited again.

And thank heaven for an efficient staff! They had prepared the schools, parents, teachers, administrators, and school board members, and then all their work fell apart. Now they went back to the problem with renewed vigor and once again came up with a great game plan. I called a few special friends, the folks who had participated in the walkout in Albuquerque. Some were from the cities we would visit. I called them for extra support and extra ideas of what to look for on our trip.

Traveling with a Nabob

We were ready, and off we went—three staff members, Randolph Hearst, and I. We knew what we had to do, but we had little idea of just what would be the best way to do it. Our visit to the various schools was as much a learning experience for us as the schools were for the kids, and appropriately enough, the best student was Randolph Hearst himself.

We hadn't gone far before he and I had tacitly agreed to drop the formality and simply refer to each other by our first names. He became Randy. I allowed him the same latitude as my buddies in Barrio Logan. I was Mando.

As travelers at government expense, our group was restricted to economical travel and lodgings. To his credit, Mr. Hearst insisted on the same accommodations we were allowed—no more, no less. Believe me, that didn't go without notice by the rest of the staff. This man was here to learn, and he wanted the full experience.

He got that experience. Our first stop was in the San Joaquin Valley, not far from Randy's stomping grounds. I'll never forget his experience at a small school. It was in the country and had only two rooms with sixty-some kids, kindergarten through grade six.

One credentialed teacher was in charge, and four Teacher Corps students from the University of Southern California did the actual classroom teaching. The Teacher Corps was the brainchild of the Office of Education and, I am convinced, a fine one. It helped students earn their certification while it alleviated the ever-present teacher shortage. I was sorry to see it curtailed some years later.

Just as we arrived at the school, right on time at 8:30, all sixty-some kids and their teachers were lined up to salute the flag. The exercise was carried out with obvious pride and with more precision than would be expected from young kids. Their clothes were well-worn but clean, and the youngsters had been freshly scrubbed before they went to school. All were poor.

Randy was impressed with the juxtaposition of penury and pride. He exclaimed, "Mando, you set this up, didn't you?"

"Sorry, Randy. I never laid eyes on these kids or on the teachers before this morning. I'd venture those little guys are rich in spirit and poor in money." I think my guest realized we had to keep one and help eliminate the other. Education would be the key.

We continued our tour, visiting schools in Stockton, Fresno, Los Angeles, and San Diego and learning something at every stop. There was one recurring problem, the one we were trying to solve: kids who couldn't speak the language of the school were at a terrible disadvantage. And they would be at a disadvantage as adult citizens in their own country because there was one, and only one, language of power in the United States—English. And it had to be standard English at that.

A kid who came through our school systems and wanted to do more than sing songs or play sports on a professional level had better be able to use the language of the country. It may have been fair or it may not have been fair, but those were the tacit rules. To become successful, people—no matter how proud they are of their heritage—had better follow those rules.

We didn't try to change them for a rich, would-be benefactor. Nor did he think we needed to. The most important thing we learned on our fact-finding tour was that even kids whose childhood language wasn't English could adapt if they were taught mostly in English. We could even preserve, as we should, the heritage of the minority. But they would have to adapt to the rules set down by the majority.

What worked best was for the minority students to be taught in English, with help for those who didn't grasp the language as well as the others. Though the amount of time students should be taught in each language couldn't be measured precisely, we concluded that teachers should stick to English for almost everything, and reserve Spanish just to clear up misunderstandings or to help kids over a spot they couldn't clear up by themselves. I borrow from the imprecise, mathematically impossible idea first used by athletes everywhere— give 110 percent. We settled for a 90/10 split—90 percent in English, and 10 percent in Spanish. And as much as possible, the 10 percent should occur after regular school hours.

Some of the folks we visited disagreed. Many felt we should simply insist on what is often called total immersion. It works in places like the Defense Language Institute in Monterey, California, where students are super-bright folks who have shown they have an aptitude for learning that is far above the average citizen's. Furthermore, they spend all their time doing nothing but learning one foreign language.

No math. No science. No social studies. In contrast, we were working with kids who spanned the spectrum of intelligence and who were trying to learn a broad range of subjects.

Indeed, some school systems did refuse to allow any bilingual education. Ironically, virtually all of them eventually ended up with the more workable 90/10 split.

Others felt we should insist on bilingual education throughout the school years. As soon as those kids learned English they would indeed be bilingual. We would encourage even Hispanic students to study Spanish in high school in order to gain a deeper understanding of where they came from. Others might want to study a third language. If they already knew two languages, the third would be even easier. Naturally, being bilingual would be asset, not a hindrance.

But our goal had to be that we were trying to turn out American citizens, ones who could compete equally in business, in politics, in industry—everywhere! That just wasn't going to happen unless the citizens we turned out could communicate in the language used by those with the power—English.

The school districts and colleges that participated in our fact-finding mission did so voluntarily. It was not an easy thing, and it did involve change, something difficult for teachers and administrators to accept. About 10 percent opted out. I was rather surprised we lost that few, and I was disappointed for each. Still, we had to keep our eye on our main goal—to find the problems and come up with ways to correct them, and to satisfy those who held the purse strings.

Now and then we were sidetracked by something completely removed from bilingual education. One incident could have been scripted by Gilbert and Sullivan. We were on campus at UCLA at the same time some Chicano students were protesting against the Coors Brewing Company for its discriminatory hiring practices.

I had too much experience with kids to take this too seriously, but it surely tested the mettle of Randy. I probably didn't help by telling some of them, "That guy is the owner of the Hearst newspapers."

What a coup! The kids could hold one of the country's top publishers hostage! And it turned out to be easy. When Randy went into a phone booth to make a call, the kids immediately surrounded the booth. They began banging on the door and shouting, "Boycott Coors!"

Randy was up to the challenge, and he told them, "I promise to never drink the stuff. I promise." The gaggle of victorious, but somewhat disappointed, kids backed away. I'm sure they had expected more resistance.

I walked away with my newly released prisoner. "Hey, Randy, you going to keep that promise?" I asked.

He smiled. "Sure, Mando. I don't like the stuff anyhow."

The thought crossed my mind that the Hearst reporter accompanying us on the trip missed a great story. Or he may have filed it but, in his wisdom, didn't run it.

Later we had another distraction—this one associated with a community group meeting in my hometown. The cops had learned that some sort of disruption was planned and wanted to send some officers to the meeting "just in case." Randy felt he had weathered a mass protest and could handle a little fuss in San Diego. But I knew some of the cops and trusted their judgment. We accepted the extra protection. The meeting, cops and all, went as planned.

Community involvement, especially involvement with parents, was one of the most important things needed in schools, but one of the most difficult for teachers to accept, especially if the parents didn't speak much English and if Spanish wasn't the native language of the teacher.

Teachers tended to hunker down (as my big boss, Lyndon, might have put it) and protect the status quo. I knew this was true because I'd been there and done that. Meeting with parents had been a requirement of my job at Gompers, and, indeed, it wasn't easy to get parents' cooperation. Nor was it easy to cope with a roomful of kids. But it is far too easy to simply try to do one's best day by day and let tomorrow take care of itself. Routine is the refuge and often the worst enemy of teachers when answers lie outside the classroom.

Meeting with teachers isn't something parents usually enjoy. That's especially true when language is a barrier. Yet nobody had a bigger stake in their kids' education than the parents themselves, and nobody held more answers to their kids' problems. We recognized this and made community involvement a priority. Always. It must be a part of any planning for education through high school.

As we went along, we came to understand what was needed and how to sell our program. Fortunately, we had help. One factor in our success was that the presence of Randolph A. Hearst attracted the attention of the media. At first, at least one reporter—usually from the Hearst chain—was with us. That helped satisfy a doubting public. Eventually we picked up much more press attention, and, thankfully, most of it was positive.

Mr. Hearst proved himself to be a good, small *d* democrat. His insistence on traveling, sleeping, and eating as a plebian set well with our crew. Mostly though, it was obvious he was a caring man, and one who really wanted to make changes for the better. He flew tourist although he could have bought the plane. Hell, he could have bought the entire airline. We stayed in good but not luxurious hotels. He ate in the coffee shops as often as not. This sort of thing made it easier for the entire staff, who would not have been able to convince their bosses of the need for such big expenditures.

We spent some time checking out the Green Valley schools, which are in the Latino area of Phoenix. We looked at their system and learned that the schools there had more success than similar schools elsewhere. The reason? They cooperated with the other schools. I doubt that Green Valley teachers were particularly smart or more able than others, but as soon as something was shown to work in one school, that method was shared with the administrators of the other schools.

This was in contrast to the methods in Tucson. Some very good results were gained by some very good teachers, but another teacher somewhere else in the same district might often be repeating the same mistakes.

This set the tone for our group. We would find out what worked, analyze it, and try to set up standards to be used as guidelines. That had been done with a great deal of success with a program operated by the University of New Mexico. Their system of tracking success was noted and eventually copied.

In San Antonio we met some people who were on their way to becoming movers and shakers in the Latino communities in America. One was Father Henry Casso, a man I'd met earlier in Washington. Father Casso was then the pastor of San Antonio's Holy Family Church and executive secretary of the national Bishops' Committee for the Spanish Speaking.

Before embarking on the tour, someone from my office, either Dean Bistline or Edna Henson, alerted the good priest of our impending visit to San Antonio. Father Casso saw an opportunity; he would hold a reception for Randolph Hearst. And what a reception it was! My friend knew how to get things done.

The executive director to the commander of Kelly Air Force Base, Sam Madrid, agreed to host the reception in his house. Strolling mariachis provided the ambiance. Members of Father Casso's parish provided food, a combination of American and Mexican dishes. Local wood-carvers and painters displayed local art. Everything bespoke the Southwest and the people who lived there. Invitations had gone out to about a hundred people, with about half expected to show up. Almost ninety did, including several prominent people.

One noted guest was Dr. José Cardenas. Dr. Cardenas had recently been selected as the superintendent of Edgewood School District, one of the poorest school districts in Texas, and he had immediately started a movement to get national funding to bring his district up to par for the area.

Of course the publisher of the *San Antonio Light*, Frank Bennack, was invited; the *Light* was Hearst's paper in San Antonio. Mr. Hearst later said it was one of the finest receptions he had ever attended. It was that and more. Frank Bennack went on to become the president and chief executive of the Hearst Corporation. He and I later received honorary doctorates together.

Over the years, Sam Madrid and José Cardenas grew as distinguished professionals and leaders. In 1994 the College of Engineering at the University of Texas, San Antonio, established as endowed scholarship in the name of Sam Madrid. José Cardenas, always with the aim of equal treatment for all, gained national recognition as a specialist in school financing.

Father Casso helped create MALDEF, the Mexican American Legal Defense and Education Fund. He later resigned from the MALDEF board to head up the scholarship and education division. His efforts were recognized by the UNESCO Paris director general, who asked to adopt the New Mexico model in Costa Rica.

Subsequently he resigned his priestly duties, married, and went on to pursue a doctorate in education. Dr. Casso is still going strong

FIGURE 13. *Left to right:* Armando, Dr. José and
Mrs. Cardenas, Father Henry Casso,
and Randolph Hearst at the reception
for Randolph Hearst in San Antonio, 1969.

as president of Project Uplift, which is dedicated to human resource
preparedness for the high technology era. He has been a strong supporter of my efforts to chronicle my life, and he has been of great help
with this book. We remain close friends to this day.

It had been quite a reception indeed!

And on we went, learning as we moved across the country. I
already had experience as a teacher and administrator. Now I was
learning how to use that experience when implementing a national
policy. I recalled my army tour of duty in Brazil in 1943. I had strug-
gled to learn Portuguese and discovered for myself the kindergarten
concept of show-and-tell. It's simply easier to learn something in
a foreign language if one can see a concrete object. I was heartened

to see teachers using this method rather than relying on using abstract ideas. They told me it worked. It ended up being included in our recommendations.

The farther we went, the more publicity we encountered. In Chicago, Hizzoner himself, Mayor Richard Daley, met us. I suspect Daley was looking for positive publicity to counter the bad publicity he'd garnered at the 1968 Democratic convention. Daley turned us over to another namesake of mine, a lady named Rodriguez. She, in turn, introduced us to the longtime superintendent of schools. He opened the doors wide, and Chicago turned out to be one of the more productive stops on the tour.

Not so down the road in Gary, Indiana. That city was beleaguered by labor problems, and that affected our quest. Hispanics were accused of taking jobs formerly held by iron and steelworkers. Unable to fight the distraction, we accomplished little and moved on to New York.

New York City, often called the melting pot of America, was certainly the melting pot of Hispanic America. Our linguistic brethren were represented by folks from Puerto Rico, the Dominican Republic, and Cuba, as well as from most other Latin American countries. All expressed a need to learn better English without forgetting their own language or setting aside their own culture.

One fascinating problem arose in south Florida. Cuban expatriates loved the idea of assimilating their kids into American society, but they also wanted us to prepare them for their return to Cuba just as soon as they toppled Fidel Castro, which would come "any day now." After all, their goal was also the goal of the president of the United States—plus his four predecessors. That was in 1969. As I'm writing this in 2005, thirty-six years and another six presidents later, Fidel Castro is still in power.

All in all, the tour was a learning experience, and we had a lot to think about. What would we do with all the information? The five of us who had just finished a long trip back and forth across the continent took a collective big breath and dived into the data we had collected. Now, how would we make this bilingual education thing work?

I decided to assemble an ad hoc committee of volunteers to prepare a proposal that would address the needs of students with limited English-speaking ability. I reviewed the names of those participants we'd recently talked to, called those that had offered the best ideas, and asked them to help. We got about eight volunteers.

At this point, I wanted to back off and let them come up with their findings and solutions without my interference. I did, however, hire a director to keep them focused. An old friend named Josué González, a Texan via Washington DC, fit the bill perfectly. He took over, and I went back to visit with an old friend in northern Virginia. A lady named Bea Rodriguez and I had a lot to talk about—maybe some other stuff as well.

Under the direction of Mr. González, the committee worked diligently for seven or eight days. The result was a proposal that addressed problems nationally, not just locally or regionally.

Now my job began. I took the various ideas contained in the proposal and pitched them to whomever would be best served by their implementation. Within two years—not bad for government work—many of our findings became policy, and full funding was picked up by Title VII of the Elementary and Secondary Education Act, also called the Bilingual Education Act. It was replaced by the measure known as No Child Left Behind.

Did all the problems we looked at go away? No. Have we resolved some? We certainly have. Will we ever overcome all of them? No, but we will know where to start when we can clear the decks and get to them, or when they become so pressing we have to do something about them. There will always be opposition to any change, and I'm willing to concede that I might be wrong, but I'll never concede that I didn't try to find a solution to the problems. That's been a goal of mine my entire life.

If we don't keep working on the problems faced by non-English-speaking students, we will leave a good part of America behind. We have to remember that in a democracy, things don't happen quickly. Our study was simply the fist step toward solving the problem. The data are still there, and will be used.

CHAPTER TWELVE

Coping with Washington Society and Its Politics, 1971–73

My stint in Washington encompassed more than the tour with Randolph Hearst. Among other responsibilities, there were the social obligations.

Living in Washington is a culture shock for newcomers to our nation's capital. Much of the work is done on a timetable with the world watching. A civil servant is not only under the scrutiny of the folks above him on the masthead, but he is also watched closely by the press, taxpayer groups, lobbyists, the opposition party, and a few dozen other varieties of gadflies.

Then there are the ceremonial honorary functions! As often as not, they are a pain for everybody involved, but no government has found a way to survive without them. When I first arrived, I was one of the few Hispanics with a grade of GS-15 or higher in official Washington. I soon learned that my value to the government went beyond my duties as director of the Office of Spanish-Speaking Affairs.

To show his appreciation, the president of the United States did something the army never saw fit to do. Lyndon Johnson gave me a medal. And I didn't have to jump on a hand grenade to earn it.

The governments of Mexico and the United States had worked out an agreement where we returned some Texas land to Mexico. A ceremony was held in El Paso, and I was chosen to attend. I'm sure my Mexican heritage had something to do with it. In any case, it was perfunctory, but Lyndon later pinned a medal on me at a White House function. I'm not denigrating it. Such pomp and ceremony is necessary, and I treasure the medal. As a matter of fact, it is hanging in a place of honor on my wall.

Then there were the dinners and social events! Washingtonians keep score by who is invited to what. A formal state dinner at the White House tops the list and rates an A+. A luncheon invitation by the president isn't far behind, maybe a B. I made the A list with a formal dinner invitation from Johnson right off. A number of luncheon invitations from Nixon followed.

The formal dinner invitation came after Bea and I had been in Washington for a few months. I rented a tuxedo, one of dozens rented for the occasion, all virtually alike. Bea went shopping for a formal. Picking out a tux was easy. There wasn't much competition for a suit that fits a guy five feet four inches tall. Bea's search for just the right formal was more difficult. What if she ended up with one identical to that worn by Lady Bird?

Of course that didn't happen, and on one of the coldest nights either of us had ever seen, two kids not long removed from Barrio Logan took a taxi to 1600 Pennsylvania Avenue to attend a state dinner in honor of the Supreme Court.

My wife was assigned to another table, so she wasn't able to help me with all the knives, forks, spoons, glasses, and dishes. I just followed what the next guy did and was lucky not to be sitting next to someone who wanted to take his cue from me.

Later, during the Nixon administration, we scored a B+ with an invitation to a luncheon at the State Department in honor of the president of Mexico, Luis Echeverría. I'm sure someone in the protocol department thought it would be appropriate for a Spanish speaker to sit next to the president, but ironically Echeverría spoke perfect English. He and I mixed the languages of two countries *de vez en cuando* (from time to time), while I took a secret delight in figuring that some noted Republican could have been sitting there in my place.

One thing you can be sure of—I did not bring up the shootings in Mexico City that occured when Bea and I visited Tlatelolco Square in 1968. Echeverría was, as I noted earlier, Mexico's minister of the interior at the time.

Bea adapted easily to Washington. Her versatility was a godsend time after time. Every step of the way, whatever came up, she made the best of it. She was always in charge of the family, and the family was better off because of it. Even when money was short, as it was for several years, she kept us fed, clothed, and out of debt.

She had worked with me as a newspaper delivery supervisor, and later helped with my political campaign. In order to make ends meet, she worked at a shoe store. In 1949 she even did a four-month stint as a riveter at Convair. Anything to help us stay afloat.

We moved five times in the first dozen years of our marriage. And all this while she was a scout leader with both the Girl and Boy Scouts. She even learned how to sew and made a lot of the family's clothes. She could spot classic American furniture under many layers of paint and refurbishing; some of her restorations became our prized furniture.

She became a top-notch cook, acclaimed by the gourmets of two families. She specialized in—guess what—Mexican food! Ironically, she did not know much about cooking even Mexican food when we first married, but she made a point of learning from one of the best, her mother, Esperanza. Then, perfectionist that she was, she didn't quit until she was cooking on a par with her mother. Now it's a family tradition that when we have a get-together, she supplies the tamales and menudo. And if the guests don't care for Mexican fare, it doesn't matter. She can whip up Italian, German, or other dishes with the best of them.

Bea and I had so much in common. We were attracted to each other in the first place because we both loved to dance, and that was easy because we were both athletic. In 1967 she tried something more typical of a blond lass from Minnesota or Massachusetts than of a dark haired girl named Beatriz. She took up ice-skating, and as you'd expect from an accomplished dancer, she mastered it.

The following spring, Bea saw a challenge she couldn't resist. She spotted an ad for tennis lessons taught by a local professional at the parks and recreation department. It didn't look that tough. After all, Maureen "Little Mo" Connolly, who was a couple years younger than Bea, had won fifty-five straight matches before her fifteenth birthday.

My wife decided to give it a go, and she assigned me an important role. I was to get her a suitable racquet. That would be easy. I'd seen pictures of Helen Wills, the great star of the 1920s and '30s, posing with a wooden racquet. So, I bought Bea one just like the great star used. Of course, Helen Wills had played years earlier, before the manufacturers discovered they could make lighter, bigger, stronger racquets out of other material. This was also before the players, but not their spouses, learned they could smash the ball better with lighter, bigger, stronger racquets.

Bea knew all that, but diplomatically didn't mention it when I proudly gave her the Helen Wills racquet. Soon, however, the wooden racquet was replaced by a new, modern, lightweight aluminum one. Neither of us commented about it, and I have no idea what happened to the heavy wooden racquet.

With the state-of-the-art equipment, Bea excelled in tennis as she had in almost everything else. She might not have ranked up there with Little Mo, but she was darn good. She played with fire in her eyes, and she couldn't be a mere dabbler, not even when her soul may have been at stake. About ten years ago, our former parish priest from Our Lady of Guadalupe Church, Father Rasura, came to visit us in Virginia. No mean player himself, when the good father found out that Bea now played tennis, he suggested they have a go at it.

Refusing to show deference to a member of the priesthood, my wife didn't cut the good father one bit of slack. She whomped him good. I'm certain she never mentioned it in the confessional either. In the confessional, one has to promise "never to do it again," and she knew she couldn't ever promise to let up at match point.

Come to think of it, Father Rasura didn't bring it up either.

A few years haven't slowed Bea down. She still plays cutthroat tennis a couple times a week with women far younger than she. Nobody cedes anything. Those young women just have to take what she dishes out.

Whenever I talk of the redeeming moments we had, I'm glad we—especially the woman who made me look good so often—got some of them in Washington.

It's becoming harder and harder to believe nowadays, but there was a time when friendship crossed party lines easily. That was the case with my friendship with one Republican in particular, William Marumoto. Marumoto, once a classmate of Nixon's at Whittier, came to the White House to take the place of David Nelson as the president's representative to oversee minority relations.

He and I have been friends ever since he arrived with the advance team to help in the transition from Johnson to Nixon. Since his job fell under the purview of HEW, he asked me to help him with a desk, clerical help, and a telephone.

Of course I was glad to help. He, an American of Japanese descent, and I, the kid from Gomez Palacio, hit it off well. He became "Bill" and I was, as always with my friends, "Mando."

Politics and business aside, Bill Marumoto was a great guy to know, and we had all sorts of fun together. We went bass fishing on the Potomac, and when time allowed, made fishing trips around the country. We attended Redskins football games together. I always suspected he was behind my invitations to White House ceremonies, including the luncheon for the president of Mexico.

Marumoto's Saint Patrick's Day parties were something to talk about, with an Irish band, great Mexican tacos, and other Irish cuisine such as sushi. (To Bill Marumoto, blurring the lines between minority groups was a good idea.) He left the administration before I did and became a headhunter—the type that makes a living finding jobs for people. In Marumoto's case, he found jobs for professionals. He's still at it, and we are still good friends.

I still had my job, but, in this case, my politics was against me. I was a Democrat in a city that would soon assume a Republican aura. After almost every election we hear of "new brooms sweeping clean." Truth is, not every member of the administration's team has to be of the same party as the president. Surely one dealing with Spanish-speaking affairs could be outside that ideology. Still, I wondered if Bea and I would again be looking for a job outside the administration. I would have worried more about staying on, except I was caught up in the fact-finding tour with Randolph Hearst. That left little time to brood about my future. When the smoke cleared, I was still there, so apparently the folks who made the decisions were happy with me.

Perhaps a bit more than happy, because in December 1970, after Nixon had served two years of his first term, I was called into the office of Dr. Sidney Marland, the assistant director of HEW. Dr. Marland offered me the job of regional coordinator of the Office of Education, a position that moved me into the so-called super grade. I would be a GS-17. This would be a tremendous job, and it was offered without considering my heritage or language.

As head of the Office of Regional Coordination, I would be in charge of the twelve regional offices scattered across the United States that managed the national education program. I would take over immediately, and the appointment would become official in March 1971.

It would be a demanding job, and to earn my keep, I had to take charge. My first question to Dr. Marland was "May I call all the commissioners to Washington for a joint meeting?"

"Of course," he replied. I had a feeling I was going to get along with my boss, at least. The meeting with the commissioners would help determine if I would get along with those working for me.

But first I was invited to a party. My staff, headed by my good friend Dean Bistline, had planned a party for me at the Mayflower, which was generally considered Washington's most prestigious hotel. And what a party it was! So many of my friends and associates attended.

Then it was back to work. I turned the Office of Spanish-Speaking Affairs over to my good friend Gilbert Chavez. Bea and I had been godparents to his daughter Crystal. I not only knew him well, but I trusted him and felt the office was in good hands.

Then came the big move—just across the hall, but a world away. One familiar thing remained, though. Dean Bistline came along. We had worked together so long that we worked almost as one. Dean would be my liaison with the folks we had to work with: the Office of Education, the State Department, school districts, universities, and all the institutions that had received federal education grants, including student loans.

Every high-ranking civil servant needs a miracle worker on his staff. Guys like Dean Bistline find mundane solutions to unsolvable problems.

We had a great staff—mostly holdovers, but they were good. We were ready to go. My first call was for the regional commissioners to come to Washington. Everybody needs to know what the new boss is like and what he expects. I intended to settle that question right off the bat. An old saying has it: "If you're going to be boss, be boss." I wanted to get that point across, but without challenging the commissioners directly.

Our meeting lasted about an hour with another hour of give-and-take questions and comments. I recognized that many of the commissioners were veterans of many years. They knew whom they could go to in order to get things done. They knew the snags of working with other departments. In short, they were invaluable.

The commissioner for the San Francisco area was Paul Lawrence. Paul and I had quite a bit in common. We had worked together for Governor Pat Brown on the Head Start program. He, like me, was a minority member, and at that time he was one of the highest ranking blacks in the state. He certainly outranked me, plus he had once held elective office, where I had failed in my only attempt. Now I had vaulted past him. Neither of us knew exactly how this might work out, so I decided to attack the problem head on. I said something like, "Paul, glad to work with you again. Let me say the most important part of my job is to help you do yours." That seemed to work, probably because it was absolutely true.

I made that philosophy a part of my operation and told all the commissioners much the same thing. I knew that as an outsider I would threaten the status quo, but I simply had to be kept in the loop. I could depend on my staff to handle most problems without my help. But few things will destroy a director's effectiveness more than the perception that he doesn't know what's going on. That's especially true when someone higher on the masthead calls down with a complaint from the field.

The commissioners and I got to know each other well in that hour or so, and even better over the next three years. I made sure they understood my main job was to help them do theirs. To this end, I kept in touch—close touch. The United States is a huge country, and I visited every one of my regional offices several times. During my stint as director, I was on the road a good 20 percent of the time.

Meeting with the commissioners headed off a lot of problems, but soon I had to deal with a big one. Ironically, it dealt with unions; I had always been a strong supporter of the right of workers to organize. In fact, from the very beginning of my teaching career in 1949, I was a member of the both the National Education Association (NEA) and the American Federation of Teachers.

When I first went to Washington, I kept my membership in NEA and was assigned a seat on its Hispanic affairs committee. Despite its high-flown name, the committee did little. At the time, I wasn't concerned because I was busy enough as it was.

In 1970 the NEA held its national convention in Detroit, and as a member, I was invited. When I learned I was to be given one of four awards for my efforts on behalf of minority children in the United States, I felt I could not accept.

When they called me to be recognized, I rose and refused the award. It wasn't so much because I personally didn't deserve it. I recognized the need for favorable publicity, but I felt that the NEA was trying to take credit for something that was obviously not a major concern of theirs, and I felt that was wrong.

My rejection stunned the crowd. I left the convention early and felt I might have been lucky to escape with my skin. Naturally, there were charges of all sorts, the most prominent being that I was reflecting Richard Nixon's dislike of the unions, especially a teachers' union.

Nothing could have been further from the truth; I simply spoke for myself. Still the animosity remained and even followed me, as I learned when I returned to work in California as president of the East Los Angeles Community College. Perhaps that's as it should be. If you don't have problems, you don't have a need for the job.

Sometimes problems come disguised as blessed events, or we may simply perceive them as problems in the first place. When we moved to Washington, we had left Christy behind to attend UCSD. In 1970 she called to tell us that she was going to have a baby and was not going to get married. On January 14, 1971, Bea and I became grandparents. I will cover this in more detail in chapter 17.

In 1972 we heard some ominous rumblings from on high. Nixon had just been reelected, and he was going to reduce the size of the government, a promise that is made by both parties in almost every election. The federal government never really gets any smaller, but some departments get whacked. It looked like mine would be one of the sacrificial lambs in 1972.

We thought perhaps it was time to say good-bye to Washington. I looked at school superintendent positions in San Diego and in San Antonio, Texas. I also looked at a job with the University of New Mexico. The San Diego job didn't look very enticing, but I wanted a job in California. I had earned many credits toward the state's retirement plan, but wasn't vested yet. Bea reminded me that our old age would be much easier to face if I would be able to have the retirement plan I'd already partially earned. But what next?

Then it happened! The Los Angeles Community College District had four vacancies for junior college presidents. One was in East Los Angeles, and it was just what I was looking for. The junior college had about fourteen thousand students, and about 70 percent of them were Hispanic. Surely a guy named Rodriguez would be given a second look.

I sent out an application and soon received a request for the deputy commissioner to interview my boss and me in my Washington office. Of course I agreed, and the interview went well enough to earn me another interview with an entire selection committee on the college campus.

The selection committee consisted of two board members, two administrators from the college, three teachers from the college, two non-teaching staff members, and one student. They didn't leave any stone uncovered!

They grilled me, and I answered their questions straight from the shoulder. I left feeling cautiously optimistic, as they say. Still, I knew there was strong competition. One fellow had all sorts of experience in college administration. Another was a popular professor and school board member with a lot of local support.

I called on a couple of my old interns, Frank Sanchez and Frank Alderete. Both were born in the East Los Angeles area. We decided that my trump card was my ethnicity. Although both Franks had been away from the school for quite a while, they made contact with one organization that they had worked with, the Association of Mexican American Educators. They urged that outfit and other similar groups to use their clout and urge the college to hire a Mexican American. The college could be the first to do so, and it was past due.

Did that do it? Who knows? It certainly didn't hurt. In 1973 I became the new president of East Los Angeles College—ELAC—and the first Hispanic to hold that position in any college in Los Angeles. Ironically, I was chosen over another very well-qualified Latino, Julian Nava, who later became ambassador to Mexico.

I was ready to start another adventure in a life filled with so many.

CHAPTER THIRTEEN

President of East
Los Angeles College, 1973–78

Temporary Washingtonians—including those of us who lived in Maryland or Virginia—always speak with disdain of living in the "zoo" (or whatever term they choose to denigrate our nation's capital).

Still, Bea and I had six exciting years there, and although we thought it a rat race at times, we liked it. When I was asked to serve in the Carter administration in 1977, we were happy to return to our nation's capital. However, back in 1972 we thought we saw the handwriting on the wall. My job appeared to be in jeopardy. About that time, I sought and accepted a job as college president; I was more than happy to leave Washington.

As often happens in our modern expanding country, our town house sold before we put up the *For Sale* sign. And again, as usual, it had appreciated enough for us to make a few bucks on it. It had been, in effect, rent-free living.

Leaving Washington involved more than just packing up and heading west. I made sure that those working for me were taken care of. I wrapped up my unfinished business, and we headed back to SoCal.

On our way, we took a detour to the northern part of our home state. We had received an invitation from Randy Hearst to visit him in a reconstructed European village on the slopes of Mount Shasta. This would be the second of four visits to my friend's retreat, and we knew we were in for a treat. Randy's father, the famous and somewhat eccentric William Randolph Hearst, had brought four chalets over from Europe and reassembled them. The chalets, plus a scaled-down version of the famous Hearst Castle, created a picturesque village. Every time we visited, we chose a different chalet.

Our four-day stay on the slopes of one of the most beautiful mountains in America was just what we needed after the rat race in Washington and before another rat race in East LA. We were right on the McCloud River. There's nothing like the gentle rippling of a river wending down a mountain to wash away the tumultuous roar of autos blaring their way through the streets of a city.

But the rest of our lives lay ahead, and our next stop was my new job. Bea and I reluctantly looked back at the snow-covered mountain as we headed south. Little did I know that my path would cross with that of Randolph Hearst again soon.

We found a beautiful, four-year-old house on a hill in Whittier, a mere four miles from the college. It was much bigger than two people would need, and the opportunities to entertain folks were fewer than we'd expected. Still, with frequent visits from Roddy, Christy, and little Armando, it was just about right.

Although my appointment wouldn't be official until later in the year, I took over the office of president from acting president John Duling. I had to get my act together and learn how to get things done in this new environment. I was lucky to inherit a couple of invaluable holdovers: Mary Kasi and Esther Renteria.

Army lore has it that a commanding officer's first job upon taking his new command should be to get to know the first sergeant, because that guy knows where the bodies are buried and what all the short-cuts are. An analogy might well be that a nascent college president should get to know the former president's secretary. She is almost bound to be as wise as ol' sarge, and likely more circumspect. I inherited a good secretary in Mary Kasi. Mary had proven staying power, having worked for all three of my predecessors. In addition to her talents, she had the admiration of everybody who worked for her. I, of course, made my own decisions, but always passed them through her to ensure we stayed on the same track.

Another godsend was Esther Renteria, who stayed on as the public relations officer. Her main function was to give a positive spin, as they say nowadays, to news from the campus. But she had a good handle on the bad news also—she was married to the assistant chief of police.

PREPARING FOR INAUGURATION DAY are member of Curriculum Adoption Network for Bilingual Biculture Education Committee, Ricardo Hernandez (seated left), Dr. Rodriguez, Dr. Jose Cardenas, and Awilda Orta. Standing are Ralph Robinette, Randolph Hearst Jr., Dr. Henry Casso, Lakie Ashford, and George Will.

Photo by Paul Colon

FIGURE 14. Newspaper clipping of Armando's inauguration at East Los Angeles College, 1973.

With two people like that working so close to me, I was free to concentrate on running the school, and that meant working through the heads of the departments, the deans. I knew they were experienced educators with a wealth of knowledge. I also knew, human nature being what it is, some might well be a bit resentful of being passed over in favor of an outsider.

As was the case when I took over the Office of Regional Coordination, I decided to meet any possible problem head on. I gave the deans a week to get organized and then invited each, in turn, to lunch. I wanted to know how the deans managed their programs, and what could be done to improve them. Mostly I wanted to get across that I was there to help them. It was a good exercise. I learned much from the series of lunches, and it forced the deans to organize their thoughts and plan for the future.

Following that, I had a full faculty meeting to let the professors and instructors know who I was and what I expected of them. Perhaps most important, I opened my office and my staff to them. If Mary or Esther couldn't solve a problem (and they almost always could), the instructor could see me personally. Most of the duties of the guy at the top involve problem solving.

Not all the problems were people problems. Managing a college with fourteen thousand students and seven hundred teachers wasn't a task to be taken lightly, especially a community college that was part academic and part vocational training. Many of the students were employed, and they attended college to learn a particular skill, often at the urging of their employers.

The size of our enrollment meant that we had to use off-campus public buildings, most of them supplied by the city, state, and federal governments. Also, the public utilities let us use their facilities, either at no cost or at very reasonable rates. In turn, we held classes aimed at teaching specialized skills to employees of the local governments.

All this enabled us to handle the large enrollment and to satisfy our commitment to the community. We even provided services to the police and sheriff departments through a program called Administration of Justice. I had several good contacts within the police department, who came in handy on one occasion.

The stage was set, and I had the duties of president before I had the official title. I was officially nominated in July of 1978 but wasn't actually inaugurated until September. The ceremony might have been a bigger deal than usual because this college with a heavily Hispanic enrollment had never before had a Latino president. Indeed, the number of Hispanics in the entire enrollment was out of proportion to the number of Hispanic deans and teachers.

The delay in being officially inaugurated didn't hurt a thing. It gave me time to become better acquainted with the school, the staff, the community, and the problems inherent in all. By the time my title was official, I was confident I could handle the job.

Ten thousand people showed up for the inauguration ceremony at our stadium. The crowd included dignitaries from all government levels—top to bottom—and education and business organizations of all sorts. Senator Cranston was there, as was my old friend and mentor

FIGURE 15. Cesar Chavez congratulating Armando at his
East Los Angeles College inauguration, 1973.

Wilson Riles. Even an old friend from yore, Cesar Chavez, showed up
to shake my hand.

It was a splendid day for the kid from Barrio Logan, and I was off
and running. There would be good days and bad days, and the bad
ones would sting. To start with, I was the new kid on the block, and
the first Hispanic in such a position. And my refusal a couple years
earlier to accept an award from the National Education Association

for contributions to minority education didn't sit well with the many union members in my college. I'd be watched carefully, and some weren't willing to give me the benefit of the doubt.

Some of my ideas were viewed with suspicion even by the folks above me in the chain of command. I had a meeting with the chancellor of the college, Leslie Koltie. I outlined my goals: raise the academic level, increase student attendance, upgrade and increase the number of buildings, expand the curriculum, increase and improve the faculty and administration, raise the level of education, and build a bridge between the college and the business community.

Chancellor Koltie told me I was biting off more than I could chew, and he was partially right. No such grandiose plan could possibly succeed 100 percent, but I would attack each and every problem. Although I didn't solve each one, I felt I improved the situation in each. I had that major motivation of knowing the chancellor was expecting me to fail. If I could pull it off, there would be the satisfaction of proving him wrong. Later he publicly lauded my term as president and apologized for giving me less than enthusiastic support.

I had a couple of important assets going for me. One was Roger Holguin. I first met Roger when he was working for the Ford Foundation, and I was in charge of the Office of Spanish-Speaking Affairs. I met him again when I was interviewing for the job as president. The young man impressed me so much as a business professor that I had him transferred to my office to help me until I felt more comfortable.

Roger was indispensable, but I had another secret weapon: my six years in Washington. I knew who could do what in the nation's capital, and how to approach that person. I would call some of my old Washington staffers to see where some grant money might be available, and then I'd fly to Washington to try to get some of it for my school.

A grant that was extremely valuable was one to build a nurses-training building. That money was allotted within a year. The modern building with extra room and modern equipment enabled us to enroll more students who wanted to become registered, vocational, or occupational nurses.

But we didn't increase enrollment for nurses' training only, and we didn't solely use federal funds. I had another asset: Esther Renteria. Early in my tenure as president, Esther and I had discussed ways to increase our total enrollment, and she was the person who did it. Her many years of experience in public relations paid off. She got editors from the two big Los Angeles papers interested in little old, mostly Hispanic East Los Angeles College.

Esther, with the help of the *Los Angeles Times* and the *Los Angeles Examiner*, developed an applications program complete with benefits and instructions for easy enrollment. It worked. Over the next couple years, our enrollment jumped from about fourteen thousand to twenty thousand. The college staff was delighted with the surge of students even though they were a burden. Still, with lots of imagination and lots of work, things came out fine.

The college also benefited from a program called Executives on Loan, which provided experts to help schools. The world was creeping into cyberspace. My office in Washington had used computers extensively, and I could see we needed them at East Los Angeles College. I applied to IBM for help, and the giant corporation came through for us.

They sent a young man to help set up programs for class selection, student assignments, teacher assignments, and record keeping of all sorts. I was, and still am, amazed at the magic of electrons to simplify so many onerous tasks. Even with the subsequent addition of new programs and new ideas, many of the original computer programs started back in 1973 are still in use today.

Later I added two ex-interns to my staff. The two Franks, Alderete and Sanchez, joined me. They had first worked with me when I was Director of the Office of Spanish-Speaking Affairs. They had guided me through the politics of getting the job as president, and they would help me run a college.

Eventually Roger Holguin, Alderete, and Sanchez became doctoral candidates through Antioch University of Yellow Springs, Ohio. I was their campus advisor, and all three received their PhDs.

A community college is a place where youngsters pick up the requisite courses for a degree. It is that, of course—and it fills that niche very well—but it's more. The college serves the community and becomes part of the community. I worked hard to ensure good cooperation between the surrounding community and its own college. We had a wide open campus. No doors were locked except those required by the insurance company.

And the community responded! Folks attended public lectures held on campus. Our green lawns were used for picnics. We respected our community, and they returned the respect. East LA is noted for its graffiti. Some entire sections of the community were "tagged" by the arcane markings of gang members. One could scarcely go a block without seeing walls and fences besmirched by the ugly markings.

Surely the acres of bare walls at the college must have looked inviting to the young kids who wanted to tell the world, "I'm here and I'm important." But we had no graffiti whatsoever on the walls of East Los Angeles College. None!

I'm proud of that, and I wish there were some sort of magic act that might curb it everywhere. I knew from firsthand experience that Latinos have a hard time assimilating into mainstream America. A graffito proclaiming LOBOS RULE! doesn't make it easier.

The commitment of our school to the community was reflected in our faculty. I tried to show my commitment to the faculty as well as the school and the community. They deserved it because they were true professionals.

Despite my generally good relationship with the faculty, one thing still rankled some of them—that damn award I had refused from their largest union, the National Education Association. I have always been a strong supporter of unions, and I relinquished my membership in NEA only because the college administration demanded it. Otherwise, my credentials as a good union member seemed impeccable, but the hard feelings remained.

During my tenure as president I oversaw many changes. Some just happened; some I made happen. Either way, the guy at the top is given the credit or saddled with the blame. It's a fact of life.

As we say in today's computer talk, IMHO (in my humble opinion), I had much more to be proud of than to be embarrassed about—the nurses' building, child-care facilities, and a big increase in enrollment. The list went on and on.

I was even appointed to the board of directors for Redlands University in nearby Redlands, California. My primary duty was to act as a liaison between the college staff and Hispanic students. It was not a mere formality, nor was it a perfunctory task.

Still, I kept hearing rumors that I was on the Redlands board for my own benefit. Some said I was after the chancellor's job. Others said that I was diverting for my own use part of the money I raised. I heard that the chancellor was going to spring a surprise audit of my accounts. He didn't, of course, but the rumors persisted. I'm happy to report that neither rumor was true.

But through it all, I had a college to run. Running a college, even a junior college, usually involves football. Football nearly always means trying to earn a spot in a bowl game. We didn't go to the Super Bowl or even the Rose Bowl, but shortly after I took over at ELAC, we did go to the Potato Bowl.

Good coaching is more important to winning a junior college football game than it is to winning the Super Bowl. Small public junior colleges don't have funds to lure supersized players. Junior college players are simply a step up from high school, and they retain most of the faults they had in high school.

ELAC had a good coach. About the time I took over as president, Al Padilla was promoted from line coach to head coach. In 1975 he took the team to the championship in the aforementioned Potato Bowl. Alas, this bowl was small potatoes, and I forget the score. Perhaps that's as it should be. There are more important things than football going on in colleges.

Not many things are more important than lifetime friendships, though. Al and I have kept in touch, and every now and then he invites me up to take part in a golf tournament.

And if you look up Potato Bowl on Google.com, you'll see that there is also a bowl game played in Grand Forks, North Dakota. I take no responsibility for any confusion. I can confuse folks on important things.

REMEMBERING PATTY HEARST

While at ELAC, I had a small part in what was one of the top stories of the early 1970s. In February 1974, I got a frantic call from my friend Randolph Hearst. I had heard that his nineteen-year-old daughter Patty had been kidnapped, and nobody knew where she was. This was terrible. One of my best friends was in trouble. As the father of a young lady myself, I suffered along with him.

Furthermore, I knew Patty personally and had such warm memories of her! I can remember one morning when I was staying at the Hearst home in San Francisco. Patty and I had breakfast together, and she initiated a long chat. She was a young lass, barely in high school; I was a middle-aged teacher, school administrator, and civil servant. But we learned from each other. After she'd been kidnapped, I often thought of that conversation. It was impossible to visualize the innocent kid as the woman who brandished a machine gun while robbing a bank.

But that February morning when I got the call, my old friend had more immediate concerns—he had a ransom note. Patty was in the hands of revolutionaries, the Symbionese Liberation Army. Soon the entire country wondered where she was. Many thought she had been taken across the border to Mexico.

"Can you help find her if she's down there, Mando?" I could feel the desperation in my friend's voice and had no answer.

But I might be able to find out. "I have some good connections in Mexico, Randy, and I'll pull every string I have."

As it turned out, I did have some pretty good strings. Manuel "Manny" Peña was an old friend whose friendship was enhanced by an ELAC program called the Administration of Justice. Manny was a cop who, like the first sergeant and my secretary, knew how to get things done. As is often the case in cities near the border, cops exchange information, officially and unofficially.

While the world pondered the whereabouts of Patty Hearst, Manny determined that she almost certainly wasn't in Mexico. That was one of the few bits of relief for her father. As long as she was alive and in the United States, he could hope for her safe return.

It soon became apparent that the good news was not really very good. The kidnappers sent a ransom note that said the young lady would be held until Randy donated six million dollars worth of food to the poor in the San Francisco Bay area. Today, Internet accounts differ on whether that much was actually delivered, but I know that some was, and I know Patty wasn't released.

The situation turned darker. The young lady joined up with her captors, and photos of her brandishing a machine gun during a bank robbery fueled the media fenzy. When she and some of the other gang members were captured a year and half after she was first abducted, she was put on trial and sentenced to jail.

Her father suffered through it all, and I suffered along with him. I remembered the sweet, innocent kid of fourteen or fifteen who could never even have done the things "Tania" (her Symbionese Liberation Army name) did.

I was back in Washington working for Jimmy Carter when the president pardoned Patty Hearst. I gave a sigh of relief that it was over at last—all except the emotional scars perhaps—and that two of my friends were able to go on with their lives.

I learned something from this. Like almost everything in the universe, right and wrong can seldom be defined precisely. Yet that's exactly what politicians promise, and we elect them because of it.

ART GALLERY

During my tenure at ELAC, I was involved in many things only peripherally related to teaching. For one thing, we were proud to be the home of the Vincent Price Art Gallery, which had been established twenty-two years earlier by the venerable actor himself. His paintings were worth millions. They were also at risk in the hot, unair-conditioned buildings. The curator, a dedicated man, wanted the gallery air-conditioned.

I agreed with the curator and thought of once again asking Randolph Hearst for help, but I couldn't always ask my old friend to bail me out. And something so prestigious and valuable to the school ought to be an expense borne by the school. The board disagreed. Boards often are loath to authorize new expenditures.

Finally I called upon every bit of diplomatic (and coercive) skills I'd learned in Washington, and the board gave in. We ended up running air-conditioning ducts from the computer room—which I'd already had air-conditioned to protect the electronic gadgets—to the nearby gallery. A little ingenuity paid off, and many irreplaceable pieces of art were given the protection they deserved.

Having air-conditioning installed in the gallery was something simple, and it was surely within the purview of the president to authorize it, but because it hadn't been done before, it caught the attention of the board of directors of the Los Angeles County Art Museum. I was nominated for and elected to a position on the board.

Ere long I met the president of the museum's board of trustees, Armand Hammer, who was also CEO of Occidental Oil and several other large corporations. Hammer sponsored three major art exhibits, and I was involved in all three: The Hermitage, from Russia; King Tut, from Africa; and Treasures of Mexico, from my native land. The kid from Palacio Gomez even managed the last exhibit. Not only that, I made sure that the entire community of East LA was invited. (I took community involvement very seriously.) I would meet with Armand Hammer again, and in dramatic fashion to boot.

CHERRY BLOSSOM FESTIVAL

In my second year at ELAC, I was asked by some community leaders if the college would host the cherry blossom festival on campus. I had no idea what a cherry blossom festival was. Still, it was a community program and thus an important thing for a community college to do.

Our new community coordinator, Art Hernandez, took charge of the details. The festival was a big deal, and Art used every available room for the many exhibits of Japanese art.

An important part of the festival was the Japanese tea ceremony, and I was invited to attend. We'd had no tea ceremonies in Barrio Logan, so this was new to me, but I gathered that politeness was the key to the whole thing. I was reduced to a game of follow-the-leader. As I had done at a White House dinner earlier, I simply followed my neighbor (Art Katayama, the co-chairman).

It went well, and I came away impressed with another custom from another culture. Later the community group gave me a beautiful painting. It sits next to a samurai metal helmet that the Asian American Business Alliance gave me in thanks for introducing them to Randolph Hearst.

A couple of years before I left ELAC, I helped some Japanese American students finance a trip to Manzanar, an internment camp in the Sierra Mountains, where some of their parents had been held during World War II. Community service was one of the best things about being president of a community college.

The two Franks and I broke new ground for colleges in the Los Angeles area. The federal government had long had a program usually called Title III. Qualified institutions, including colleges, could apply for a grant that could be used for programs chosen by the institution, subject to approval by the regional offices, of course. It was like money in the bank. But nobody in our area had applied for a grant like this before.

Frank, Frank, and I did just that, and bought ourselves yet another project. It was a hassle to go through the grant process because it was new, but finally we had our money. Then everybody wanted some. Our college became the go-to place for help in applying for a Title III grant.

Nothing like creating even more work for yourself.

APPOINTED COMMUNITY SERVICE

Before I left ELAC, I was appointed to a local committee to make political recommendations. Many of our deliberations and recommendations can be found in a report entitled "To Serve Seven Million," published a few years later.

At that time, the Los Angeles Board of Supervisors consisted of five members. Citizens in our area were left with little voice in their own city. Our committee tried to increase the number on the board with members from the East LA area. We recommended two new supervisors. That didn't fly, but some borders ended up being changed, and Gloria Molina, a one-time ELAC student, has been supervisor since 1991. As a woman and as a Hispanic, Gloria broke her own ground, but I'd like to think our report had something to do with it.

And so it went. I served on several boards. One was the board of KCET-TV, the public broadcasting station for Los Angeles. I was also on the board of the United Way and was a member of the Reform of Intermediate and Secondary Education (RISE) Commission, as well as many others.

Mando, the Movie Star

The kid from Gomez Palacio via Barrio Logan had done pretty well, being a principal of both junior and high schools, working at high levels in both the state and federal governments, and now serving as president of a college. What could be next?

How about being a movie star? If I made it, could I be a hero? Could I make the young ladies swoon? A far-fetched, wacko idea? Sure, but believe it or not, I had my shot, sans swooning.

I was approached by two professors who were shooting a film to be used in a Mexican history course at Valley College, one of the schools in the San Fernando Valley. The professors needed a swarthy-looking dude to play Benito Juárez, Mexico's first indigenous president.

Unlike most heroic figures, Juárez was indeed swarthy. That meant I'd get to be a hero, not some dark-skinned guy who shot the hero. I was honored to represent him on the big screen. Juárez, who served two terms in the mid-1800s, is often regarded as Mexico's greatest and most beloved leader. He was president on May 5, 1862, the date of Mexico's famous victory over the French. That day is celebrated throughout southern California and Mexico as Cinco de Mayo.

In the film, I portrayed Juárez as a younger man, when he was a sheepherder. I had about three hundred words of dialogue. I've been waiting for another casting call ever since.

I'm now an old man and can look back on a lifetime of work and service. No stint was more difficult than trying to hold down all the wildly varying aspects of being president of a community college. And I don't think anything was more satisfying.

CHAPTER FOURTEEN

Back to the
Seat of Power, 1978–83

Running a community college was satisfying in so many different ways. It was certainly satisfying when the chancellor grudgingly admitted I'd done better than he had expected. But my relationship with the largely Latino community was probably even more satisfying. At one point there was a 50 percent increase in the number of local kids attending our community college than had attended before I took over.

Education, more than anything else, is the key to opening doors beyond the barrio. I learned that from my own experience, and I was glad to help broaden the opportunities for more kids.

While I was at ELAC, the multi-talented Bea, as always, was indispensable whether she was presiding over a gourmet dinner or helping me keep in touch with the students and their problems. She was especially helpful with the tennis teams. She had learned to be a top-notch player in Washington, and her skills came in handy on the courts of ELAC.

Bea assumed an unofficial role as assistant coach and shared her knowledge of the game with the young ladies. In addition, she would go along on road trips as a chaperone. Best of all, as she adopted the tennis players, they adopted her.

My job satisfaction didn't end with my duties as president or the duties taken on by my wife. My extracurricular activities competed with my duties as an educator in so many ways. I learned from both, but as president I was primarily an educator. Helping maintain an art museum taught me more about art than I ever knew before. I learned to fake my way through a Japanese tea ceremony. I even had a nodding acquaintance with finance because of a short stint with the Federal Reserve Board.

Ironically, it was one of those extracurricular activities that lured me away from the college and back to Washington. Like Americans of most ethnic groups, many Mexican Americans celebrate the national holidays of their ancestral home. Each September 16, the folks in East LA celebrate Mexican Independence Day, and the ELAC president is usually named chairman of the program.

In 1976, an election year, we invited the men atop both of the national tickets, President Gerald Ford and his challenger Jimmy Carter, to participate. We weren't sure how we'd handle it if they both accepted, but we knew it would be such a coup that whatever we did would garner us favorable publicity. President Ford took care of our problem. One look at the demographics convinced him he could get more votes elsewhere—not many Republicans in East LA.

Our area did have lots of Democrats, but the trick was to get them to vote. Carter accepted our invitation, and we rolled out the red carpet. I had the opportunity to escort him to various functions and to have long, informal talks with the man who was soon to become the most powerful person in the world. The celebration was by all accounts a big success. I like to think that I once again helped elect a president.

Some months after the inaugural, I heard from President Carter. A staff officer sent me a memo asking if I'd be interested in a position in Washington. I was flattered, but I had left Washington only five years earlier, and things were going well in East LA—my job was a heady experience. I sent a polite but unenthusiastic reply, thanking them for the offer, but saying, "No thanks this time." I was still politician enough to leave the door open a crack.

It turned out that I was fortunate I hadn't slammed the door harder. A tax revolt loomed. One of California's infamous propositions was in the works. Proposition 13 would roll back property taxes and make other tax measures difficult to pass. The proposition was still down the road, but the harbingers were in the air. By 1978 state funding of public facilities, especially schools, was sharply curtailed. Already there was a scramble for funds. It got personal and it often degenerated into the friend-against-friend stuff.

About that time, I received another letter from the Carter administration. This time I was asked to consider being an assistant secretary of the Treasury Department, a job I knew absolutely nothing about. Oh sure, there'd been that job as an advisor to the local office of the Federal Reserve Bank, but that was more as a liaison with minority, principally Hispanic, communities. I would be completely out of place in the world of high finance. I sent another letter begging off.

I was reconciled to staying on at the college and fighting the good fight, when I got yet another letter. This time I was offered the position of a commissioner of the Equal Employment Opportunity Commission (EEOC). Hey, that was right up my alley! I jumped at the chance to return to Washington.

This job would be a significant step upward, and with it came new scrutiny—I had to have a security clearance. That meant I had to pass an investigation by the FBI. To start with, I had to list every place I had lived and every job I had held.

Jobs! My God, there had been so many, starting with selling shards of ice and ending with being a college president! I was proud of all of them. Unfortunately, that meant I had to remember them. I also had to remember each place I had lived in fifty-five years. We had owned five houses and had rented several times that many. It took me a good three weeks to assemble all the information needed.

Finally, convinced that even my residence in a dusty town in central Mexico didn't equate with communism, the FBI gave me its imprimatur, and I was ready to be confirmed by the Senate. During the confirmation hearings, nobody had any particularly bad things to say about me, and three local congressmen—Senator Alan Cranston and Representatives George Danielson and Lionel Van Deerlin—had nice things to say. It took the entire Senate less than an hour to put its own imprimatur on me.

Now for the formalities. I was to be sworn in as a member of a national commission. The head of the EEOC, Eleanor Holmes Norton—who was also my future boss—came out to Los Angeles to officiate. At my request, the ceremony was held in Los Angeles so my family could attend. We used the courtroom of Judge Robert Takasugi, and my family got the best seats—the jury box. It was a good thing they did because the courtroom was filled.

More formalities followed, the best of which was a dinner organized by the community college district office. Someone asked me if I had a preference as to where I would like to have the dinner. Boy, did I!

Thirty-five years earlier I had been turned away from the Los Angeles Athletic Club in downtown Los Angeles. Of course, I wasn't a commissioner in a government agency then. At the time, I was a member of the Neighborhood House wrestling team, an eclectic team with blacks, Hispanics, Asians, and even some Anglos. When we had tried to enter through the front door, we were stopped and told to go around back to the service entrance. In 1941 use of the front door to the athletic club was restricted to whites only. Now I was a commissioner in a government agency aiming to wipe out discrimination. Could there be a better venue for emphasizing equal opportunity?

These thirty-five years later I don't remember exactly what I said, nor do I have a copy of the speech, but, in part, it went something like this:

> The offer to become a commissioner of a group dedicated to fighting discrimination was the second offer I had to join our new administration in Washington. I turned down the first, an offer to be assistant secretary of the Treasury. I declined it because I didn't know that much about finance.
>
> But discrimination, *that* I do know something about. As a Hispanic nicknamed Shadow, I understand the problems one can experience in America by having dark skin. Thirty-five years ago, I and an entire wrestling team were turned away from the front door of this building because most of the wrestlers on our team had dark skin—some as dark as mine, some as black as ebony. I think one or two of the guys might even have been white.
>
> I am glad to point out that the Los Angeles Athletic Club changed their policy years ago, and I want to emphasize that they did it without pressure.
>
> Other venues across our country aren't as eager to open their doors to all Americans, especially Americans of color. That's why those of us of color and with ancestors who didn't

come here from northern Europe must constantly stand up for our rights. That's why we have an Equal Employment Opportunity Commission.

That wasn't the end of my talk, of course, but I was glad to get something off my mind. Perhaps as important, I was glad to be able to say it exactly where it was so appropriate.

Now I was indeed on my way to Washington. *Dicho y hecho* (said and done).

BACK TO WASHINGTON

We were on the way back east. It's a long drive from Los Angeles to Washington DC, but it was autumn, and we would be going past many of the EEOC's district offices. This would give me the opportunity to do what I always do—get to know the people who worked for me. We mapped out our trip and planned stops in regional or area offices in Phoenix, El Paso, Dallas, and Memphis.

I did not look for problems or even think about changes. That would have to wait. I wanted merely to show my face, get to know the folks I'd be working with, and gain a greater understanding of what I'd be facing down the road.

The only particular difficulty we had was in Knoxville where we stayed in the same hotel with some Tennessee Volunteers fans. The Tennessee fans stayed up most of the night whooping it up with declarations of how they were going to whup them Kentucky Wildcats. Those folks from Appalachia can make a lot of noise at football season. Maybe at other times, too, but we spent only one night in Knoxville.

Bea and I talked about how nice it was to be laid-back Californians. With the possible exception of University of Southern California fans, Californians don't get worked up over things like that. In any case, our trip east was a pleasant one, and I arrived in Virginia with a better understanding of my new job.

A nip was in the air, but the snow hadn't started flying yet, and we had our house waiting for us. Anticipating the move, Bea and I had made a couple earlier trips to check out the homes. On one trip, Bea visited an old tennis friend who was also a real estate agent. She showed us some houses in the area, and we bought the third one we saw.

We arrived at our new address an hour before the van came with our belongings. My wife and I directed traffic, and as soon as everything was in place, we made our first new friends in the neighborhood, Murphy and Edith Wright. Edie brought over some sandwiches.

We were to spend the next thirteen years living about a half mile from Mount Vernon, the residence of George Washington. Our house, however, was quite a bit newer than George's. Built in 1970, it was part of a homeowners' association with rules. I didn't find an unreasonable rule among them. Our community was as integrated as any in that neighborhood and much more integrated than parts of San Diego County even today.

One of the most significant days in my life took me by surprise. Back in Los Angeles, I'd been sworn in by Judge Takasugi, but becoming a commissioner appointed by the president meant I had to be sworn in again, this time by Vice President Walter Mondale. I learned on a Tuesday that the ceremony would be held in only forty-eight hours. I wouldn't have enough time to notify all my friends and family.

By Thursday I had managed to round up Bea and a few friends, but so many others couldn't come on such short notice. The United States of America was represented by my former boss at the Office of Education, Serena Bloom; Secretary of the Treasury William Miller; and President Jimmy Carter.

The next day I went back to work. I was a new executive, sworn in by the veep. For all that, it was about the same as every other job I ever had, at least at first. I had to get organized, learn my place in the pecking order, and assemble a staff. Some things just never change.

I had my duties to perform, and the holdovers from the previous commissioner helped keep me going until I filled the positions with my own people. First I had to get someone to run the office, take care of all the details, and keep me out of trouble—another first sergeant, if you will. I contacted a capable secretary I knew from years earlier, but after being in the Office of Education so long, she was simply too valuable there to start all over in EEOC. A subsequent search turned up Leonore Corpus who fit the bill to a *T*. She stayed with me as long as I stayed in government service.

FIGURE 16. Beatriz, Armando, and President Jimmy Carter, 1978.

My organizational chart called for a lawyer. I guess I was finally important enough to need one. I asked around the department, and one name popped up almost every time: Segismundo Pares. He was in our Denver office and was considered one of the best.

Although Mr. Pares had worked in our Denver office, he traveled to Washington quite often. On one of his trips, I cornered him, interviewed him, and offered him a job in Washington. He accepted, and I ended up with an excellent legal advisor. I dubbed him "Siggie" because a name like Segismundo didn't trip lightly off the tongue.

Having people in our department who spoke a foreign language was a big advantage because so many of our patrons were recent immigrants. Siggie spoke several languages. Not only that—his writing in English was impeccable.

FIGURE 17. Armando and his staff of Equal Employment
Opportunity Commission; Segismundo Pares
second from left and Dean Bistline at far right, 1978.

He hailed from Cuba, where he was once a classmate of another
Cuban of note, a fellow named Fidel Castro. Siggie left the country
when his fellow alumnus came to power. Old school ties go only so
far when dealing with revolutionaries.

Our Cuban had earned a law degree in Havana, but it was worth
little more than the paper it was printed on. Cuban law, turned on its
head by Castro's firing squads, was suspect in Siggie's new country.
American law was something quite different. Not to be denied his
chosen profession, he ended up getting an American law degree at a
college in Birmingham.

I held on to him for my entire tenure at EEOC. He was not only a
hardworking staff member, he was one of the most interesting people
I have known. My understanding of that enigma ninety miles off our
coast was enhanced by our many conversations. Just as I was putting these words down, I learned that he had passed away in 2004.
I'm sorry he is gone. He was one of the really good guys who passed
through my life.

And there was my old colleague Dean Bistline, who was then working for the California Department of Education in Sacramento. I again lured him east to work as my chief of staff.

A quasi-official requirement in EEOC was that commissioners had to withdraw from all organizations where we might have a conflict of interest. I cut loose from the California Teachers Association, the National Education Association, and the Urban League, among other organizations. Officially, I was now an enemy of the outfits I'd supported so enthusiastically for so long.

Early in my second stint in Washington, I received my second reminder that I was not always in control of my body. My first reminder had been when I had that bout with asthma while serving in the army. I had compensated by changing my lifestyle. I quit football, stopped smoking, and avoided lots of foods. In 1979 my reminder was more poignant, and I came to realize that, no matter what, I was mortal.

That was the year my old friend and comrade from the political battles of southeast San Diego, George Walker Smith, was being seated as the president of the National School Boards Association. Because I had been his successful campaign manager in his first run for office, he invited me to be the keynote speaker.

Bea and I were off to San Francisco, where all went relatively well at Smith's installation. When Randy Hearst learned I was in town, he asked Bea and me to accompany him and some friends on a fishing trip off Baja. I asked for a few days leave, and we were off to Baja.

I knew that when Randy was involved, any enterprise—even a fishing trip—would be top-notch, and this started out to be exactly that. Randy was a good friend of Abelardo Rodriguez, son of Abelardo Rodriguez, the Mexican president from 1932–34. The elder Rodriguez owned the island, and his son gave us the use of Bing Crosby's old vacation home there.

Things were still going well the first night. Desi Arnaz of TV fame hosted a reception for our group. Then Bea and I spent the night in the Crosby cottage. The next morning we boarded the fishing boat and were on our way to catch some big ones, when I was reminded of my mortality.

"Look, Mando! There are wild goats up on that hill," said Bea.

I quickly turned my head to look, but never saw a goat. I simply fell to the deck, out cold. I recovered soon and felt okay. But a blackout like that was bad news for a guy approaching sixty. Randy and Bea insisted I get checked out. Randy had the boat turn around to return me to Rodriguez Island. A doctor was vacationing on the island, so Randy summoned him to examine me.

The doctor's advice was for me to return to the States for a complete checkup. Then Abelardo Rodriguez Jr. flew me to Cabo San Lucas, where we caught a plane to Los Angeles. My doctor there advised me to return to Washington, where the Veterans Administration had my complete records.

From there I was returned to my personal doctor. He determined that my carotid artery was twisted, which intermittently cut off the blood supply to my brain. I had an operation to untangle the thing. I spent a week in the hospital and then returned to work. For a while, my mind ran ahead of my ability to express myself. But all in all, it was a success.

My doctor told me that my condition wasn't unusual, and it was relatively easy to correct. I suppose he was right, but when someone slits my throat, even to repair something, I am reminded that I'm here on this planet for only a while.

As I've noted, working at a relatively high level in Washington involves much more than what a job description might call for. There's always the politics, even for a civil servant.

After I recovered from surgery, the decks were cleared for action, and I was ready to dive in headfirst. Commissioner Eleanor Holmes Norton was a great boss. She knew her business, expected you to know yours, and backed you up as long as you stayed within the lines. Rules meant something to that lady!

I learned about the rules early in an embarrassing incident. One of my close relatives used my name to try to get a job within EEOC, which was a violation of the rules. I would have stopped him, but I had no idea what he did until Ms. Norton called me into the office and explained it to me. I apologized and accepted responsibility. Then I confronted the person, asked him to withdraw, and that was that.

As far as possible, all commissioners on Ms. Norton's staff were given assignments that would benefit from their expertise. Although

I was not (and still am not) a computer nerd, at the 1964 New York World's Fair, I did recognize computers' potential. A few years later, I dare say I jumped out ahead of the curve when I had an extensive computer system installed at East Los Angeles College. Ms. Norton gave me my first task at EEOC, which was to develop a program that would put a dent in the paperwork inherent in a Washington office.

We did it too—at least until more and more records took up the extra space in the computers. Paperwork, even when it isn't on paper, will always proliferate in our nation's capital. But it was a good start, and in an expanding and changing Washington, computers were becoming essential.

Computers would be a big part of my life. In an ever-changing country such as ours, a problem solved or a situation improved becomes a standard for future problems in other areas. I was pleased to see our efforts eliminate a lot of waste and save money. I was especially pleased to see our efforts echoed in other areas of our department.

Soon I was being assigned to chair meetings to review and select cases that would be presented to the full commission. I was assigned interagency meetings as well, and one of them was under the aegis of the attorney general. It was a great one. Along with representatives of every major government agency, we tried to make a coordinated effort to tackle the problems of the physically disabled. For instance, all government agencies should have the same rules. A person bound to a wheelchair but otherwise capable is going to have the same problems at the Department of Defense as he or she will at the State Department.

One particularly tough problem we dealt with was language discrimination. Most Americans speak only English. The exception would be the folks who need help the most—immigrants or folks who live apart from mainstream America. English is complicated enough for native-born Americans. For those who know it as a second language, the problem is magnified. Slang or a nuance can change the intended meaning. That's especially true if something is taken literally, as a subordinate is likely to do.

On the other hand, employers certainly must feel justified in requiring their employees to speak English in the course of their duties. We didn't solve the problem nationwide, of course, but we did determine that the major problems weren't between boss and worker, but between the workers themselves.

I suppose it's human nature that when folks hear someone else speaking a language they themselves don't understand, they tend to assume that the other person is talking about them. At a worksite, those situations put the boss in the middle. In the end, we didn't solve those problems because each case was different and so pervasive. We did understand it well enough to let staff workers handle it.

Believe me, language is a problem, even for those of us who are supposed to understand it. While working at EEOC, I gave a speech in Denver in which I made reference to the misunderstanding of the Spanish word *huevo*. As any high school kid who has taken Spanish knows, that word means *egg*. But as any kid from the barrio knows, *huevos* (always plural in this context) often has a different and vulgar connotation. Context is important.

Here we had a Mexican American speaking to a mixed group of Hispanic attendees and reporters. One Anglo gleaned enough from it to be offended, even though the comments were germane for that subject and that audience. She wrote a piece for the *Denver Post* complaining about my lack of tact.

This is the sort of thing that can harm a government official of any sort. I immediately apologized for the misunderstanding, but that ended up sounding like weasel wording. I hadn't needed to apologize. Almost everybody except that one reporter understood the point I was making, and so many defended me that it all passed without further ado. I was lucky—many careers have been ruined by such things.

An issue as contentious as language is immigration, especially illegal immigration. It has long been a big concern in the United States. Various "solutions" have been offered. Some of the same ones keep popping up: seal off the border, but only the southern border; patrol the border with volunteers; open up the Mexican border much as we have done with the Canadian border.

All those "solutions" have something in common—they won't solve anything. Maybe some will alleviate the situation, but illegal immigration will still exist as long as we have a rich nation next to a poor one. Thousands of willing, sometimes desperate workers are willing to do what is often called stoop labor for less pay than the

Americans. Few Americans are willing to do those same jobs, but the American consumer likes the savings gleaned from cheap labor.

And everybody complains.

We focus so much on illegal immigration here that we tend to assume it's strictly an American problem. Not so at all! It is a world-wide problem. As long as there have been borders, there have been problems with illegal immigrants. It's so pervasive a problem that the United Nations scheduled international conferences to address it. I was the U.S. representative to two of them: one in Vancouver, British Columbia, in 1979; and the other in Italy. In 1980 Bea and I traveled to San Gimignano in the mountains of Tuscany, about thirty miles from Florence, Italy.

Americans wonder what to do about folks coming over our southern border. In many cases, Europeans are concerned with borders on all sides. So many countries in such a small space! So many different languages! Any sort of economic downturn in a neighboring country looses a horde of workers from that country, their allegiances left behind.

No group epitomized that situation more than the Gypsies, those nomadic people with no national allegiance. As are so many Latinos in the United States, the Gypsies are disparaged throughout Europe. The names given them bespeak contempt, especially in the Netherlands and Germany, where they are called "Heathens."

Gypsies are a largely illiterate tribal group whose language can be traced back to India whence they came via Egypt. They have long been thought to live outside the general rules as much as possible. Seldom can one find a record of any of them paying taxes. Those few whose children attended school didn't share the cost in any respect. The burden of local police officials who tried to keep an eye on them was borne entirely by the local citizens. They have a worldwide reputation, probably overblown, for being thieves. I never saw any documentation of this.

The UN meeting awakened me to the fact that America's problems are simply a reflection of the world's problems. And like them, we aren't open to the quick solutions promised by politicians. We simply have to keep trying.

But our stay in Italy wasn't all work. In San Gimignano Bea and I were in a nearly authentic medieval community. Not much had changed since it had flourished in the beginning of the fifteenth century. San Gimignano was a city of fewer than four thousand people with ten-foot-high walls surrounding it and cobblestone streets.

About once a week, merchants from town and farmers from surrounding areas set up a mobile market. Bea swears she could buy anything there. It certainly seemed so—clothes, produce from the surrounding farms, magazines, papers, and some of the most delicious wine on earth. You could even get a haircut or a permanent in mobile barber shops or beauty parlors set up right there on the street. Each Tuesday evening, some thirty young men dressed in medieval costume put on a spectacular show complete with bugles blaring and flags waving.

We loved it.

All that and I didn't get away from the United States on our getaway. While heading to the train station in Florence I heard, "Hey, Shadow!" It was an old friend from Barrio Logan. I suspect he had forgotten my name as I had his.

About the time Bea and I got back to Washington, my boss was replaced by a boss of a different political party. Ronald Reagan would want his own man as chairman, so Eleanor Holmes Norton would be out. But what about the rest of us? A lot depended upon who replaced her. Who would it be?

It turned out that my new boss was a relatively unknown attorney, but one with a good reputation. His appointment was considered a move up from his position as an assistant secretary for civil rights with the Department of Education. His confirmation as chairman of EEOC was very routine compared with his confirmation eight years later as a justice of the U.S. Supreme Court. Clarence Thomas would be my new boss.

Things at EEOC went along well and, by and large, I—a lifelong Democrat—worked well with a conservative Republican. Thomas was not as demanding as Norton had been, nor were his instructions as precise, so there was great opportunity for error.

Most of the time we worked well together, but not always. One thing bothered both me and Tony Gallegos, my old friend from Los Angeles. Tony was, like me, a lifelong Democrat, but he had split from his party and supported Reagan over Carter. When Reagan won, he brought Tony into the administration as a commissioner of EEOC.

Tony and I were concerned that the complaint filings from the Hispanic community were much lower than should be expected, given the number of Hispanics in the country. We both came from the barrio and simply didn't believe things had somehow changed that much for the better when we moved to Washington. Something had to be amiss. We asked that our commission conduct a study to see what was going on.

Thomas disagreed and refused to order the study. That wouldn't do! We knew EEOC was not adequately representing the millions of Hispanics in the United States, and we both knew from experience that Hispanics had problems whether complaints were filed or not. The problems would not go away, and they would eventually be the country's problems. So despite the boss's disapproval, we stuck to our guns and rounded up support from our committee.

Then I brought the issue up as an agenda item, and it passed over Thomas's dissenting vote. He had to go along with the vote, but he didn't have to fund it. As planned, our study was to take us to many different cities to look at various problems—a difficult task without money. We would simply have to make do with whatever we could scare up from our own budgets.

But then I thought of another way, one that my boss could not stymie. I had lots of contacts among employers, union leaders, and other interested parties. They provided enough money to get the study started. We cut some places from our schedule and kept the bigger, more volatile ones. We heard enough testimony to confirm that EEOC, while doing a good job ensuring that blacks were included in opportunities, was simply not extending its services to the Hispanic community.

Indeed, by the time we got to the last two venues for our study, Thomas himself had come around. He even attended the meetings as an active participant. The upshot of our efforts was that Hispanics' problems were actually included in EEOC studies. It was ironic that a problem that had started under Democratic administrations was corrected by a Republican administration, with the help of a couple of notable Democrats.

Although it had not been my intention to pick a fight with the head of the outfit, my decision to "fight" Thomas turned out to be the right decision. Clarence Thomas, to his credit, also made the right choice. He refused to ease me out when my tenure was up. He specifically asked me to stay on until a replacement could be found.

Years later, when he was undergoing such intense scrutiny in his confirmation hearings, I was besieged by the press asking whether I knew of his alleged sexual misconduct. Even though I knew both him and Anita Hill well, I honestly answered that I did not know of any sexual misconduct.

I left federal government service for good on October 1, 1983, but there were still many other things to do before I finally called it quits and retired.

CHAPTER FIFTEEN

Retirement Doesn't Mean
Not Working, 1983–2001

As October 1983 approached, I started to get nervous. One last good-bye party and then I'd walk out the door, retired and unemployed for the first time since before I had sold shards of ice from my wagon in Barrio Logan. What would I do next? I'd heard of so many who spent most of their lives working hard, and then when they retired, they just died. The trauma of a big change like that causes the mind to work in mysterious ways.

As it turned out, it was a needless worry. I didn't die, and I didn't stay idle—not even for a single day. Within a few days of my retirement, I received all sorts of offers from folks who would keep me so busy I wouldn't have time to die or even rest.

The most notable call came on my birthday, September 30. It was also one day before I was "piped over the side" for the last time as a civil service officer. My old friend Randy Hearst wanted to share an idea he'd been kicking around ever since our cross-country tour back in 1969. Computers had revolutionized Randy's world, the newspaper industry. By 1983 computers were poised to revolutionize the entire world.

That brought forth a question. What would all this mean to education? Would kids be able to cope in this modern world of computers? Most likely the children of affluent parents would manage; they would be able to do their homework on the things because their parents could afford to own home computers. That would probably be to the relief of teachers from coast to coast. Could teachers be fair in judging the work of two students if one presented a neat, nicely typed paper, and the other handed in an essay that had been scrawled in pencil on a lined pad?

And reference materials! Internet connections and powerful search engines like Google weren't yet common, but a kid with a computer would have many, many more references readily available than would kids without computer access. Parents could buy software containing the *Encyclopaedia Britannica* with articles accessible by a mouse click. How much of an advantage would that be over having to find an actual encyclopedia and then leaf through a couple of volumes? Which kids would be able to move from school right into a world practically run by computers?

Those were some of the questions that bugged my old friend, but there were more. Randy had an overriding concern that I might have engendered. During our cross-country trip a decade earlier, I had introduced him to a world he hadn't actually come face-to-face with—a world where inner-city kids of America often found that their world ended at the edge of their neighborhood.

My friend had in mind a pilot program to see how computer-training programs could enhance education, and he wanted my help. I knew the Department of Labor was already working on such a project, but there was so much to be learned—the government and a private enterprise could complement each other. This project was right up my alley, and I'd be able to work with one of my favorite people. No way could I refuse. In fact, I'd been thinking along the same lines myself, and his call gave me an idea.

"Randy, I think this is something your grandmother, Phoebe, would want you to pursue. For much of her life she tried to get kids, especially disadvantaged kids, interested in education before they simply slipped into 'their place in society.' I am an example of education that started early and worked. You can carry on your grandma's work, and I can help other kids who are much like I was."

Surely I didn't need Grandma Phoebe to sell the program, but my knowing what his grandmother wanted didn't hurt a bit. Best of all, it was absolutely true.

To ensure that we reached our target group—disadvantaged kids—Randy and I felt we should focus on schools in the inner city. San Francisco and New York, major hubs for the Hearst Corporation, would be ideal. Next we had to determine at what grade level we would start. First grade? Fourth? Perhaps even kindergarten? Maybe even preschool?

We made our first tentative approach to kindergarten teachers and were met with some resistance. Some thought that kindergarten was simply too early in life to work with computers. Perhaps, but we were trying to learn, not simply to accept what we already believed.

I felt that if we could start teaching kids to do simple things with pencil and paper, we could also teach them how to do simple things with a keyboard. After all, we just wanted the kids to use the things, not build them. We stuck to our guns and eventually won over the doubters.

About this time, I realized that although twice I had helped offices install extensive computer systems, I lacked basic computer skills myself. So it was back to school for Tio Mando. I took a class where I learned not only how to run the things, but how to teach others to run them.

It was the best training program I'd had for ages, and I still use my computer skills daily, although the field is changing so rapidly that I'm constantly amazed at how much I don't know. I'm also amazed at how much information there is a mere mouse click away. It was imperative that we bring our kids the modern technology of computers.

By early summer of 1984, we launched our program at two schools in San Francisco: Bret Harte Elementary, with a predominantly black enrollment; and George R. Moscone Elementary, where most of the kids were Hispanic. About the same time we launched another program in New York City's Public School 33, which had mostly black kids.

Fortunately, the principals and administrators at all the schools gave us their cooperation. The idea of being on the cutting edge of technology while having the influence and resources of the Hearst family was a tremendous incentive.

It wasn't easy. Classes had to be shifted so that seven grades (kindergarten through grade six) had access to computers. Hearst had to buy the computers, and then we had to find space for them. The schools each needed an extra teacher, so we had to train and assign a computer specialist in addition to the regular classroom teachers. They all worked together to teach the class.

We could see it worked. The use of computers enhanced learning across the board, but this was a pilot program, so we needed proof.

There we fell short because the student population at both schools shifted so much that we couldn't track the program.

Although our three schools didn't provide the proof we needed for the Hearst Foundation to continue the funding, we were making progress, and we were learning. We stuck with the three original schools and looked elsewhere for an ideal place where we could confirm our findings.

I nosed around and came up with Bakersfield, north of Los Angeles. The school district met our two major criteria—the students were from low-income households, and the families were stable, so the student population didn't change much.

The administration of the Bakersfield schools wasn't as stable. I was initially attracted to Bakersfield because I knew the superintendent, Dr. Herb Cole. But before we could get things off the ground, he left. His replacement worked well, but she too was recruited away. Finally, an old friend of mine ended up in the job.

I had known Dr. John Bernard in San Francisco, and he was familiar with our program at Bret Harte Elementary. We worked together for years, enough to get the program off the ground and running. First we set up shop at Bakersfield's Josten Elementary School. There we gathered the data to satisfy the Hearst Foundation so they would continue to fund our project.

Securing funding for our project was one of the objectives of moving into Bakersfield. With that objective met, we became involved in another project: "Baby Steps." Around 1990 the city of Bakersfield appointed the principal of Longfellow Elementary School, Jan Hensley, to be director of the Child and Development Program. She developed a plan called "Baby Steps." In many ways, it anticipated 1998's Proposition 10, a proposition spearheaded by actor Rob Reiner. Ms. Hensley and, later, Reiner were convinced that the children were even more receptive to learning at an early age.

This idea was so similar to what we were trying to do with the Hearst Foundation that it was inevitable that Ms. Hensley and I would end up working together. Not that working together was a new experience for us; we knew each other from Josten Elementary, where she had been vice-principal.

Hearst donated $150,000 to help the city of Bakersfield set up

Ms. Hensley's program in the East Hills Shopping Center. This was not a computer education program, although computers were added later. It was for kids, and it worked—and still does. Ms. Hensley and I kept in touch until 2001 when Randy Hearst died and the Hearst Foundation stopped its affiliation with the program.

When Reiner's Proposition 10 passed, the Bakersfield plan was the first one funded by the cigarette tax. The program still continues, and Baby Steps is still the baby of its founder.

Randy Hearst wasn't the only person who offered to keep me from a retirement filled with ennui. I soon learned that almost everybody needed a person who needed something to fill his hours—at no pay of course.

I am an American, and I consider myself to be American in all respects. Still, I speak Spanish and look more like a typical resident of Mexico City than of Alexandria, Virginia. After living more than eight decades and achieving some success, I still don't know whether being Latino is an advantage or a disadvantage—but sometimes, it made me more valuable than a six foot four, blond Anglo. My involvement with United Community Ministries is an example of that.

Just about the same time as Randy's call in 1983, I received one from Mrs. Sharon Kelso, the director of United Community Ministries. UCM was a social service group, funded by the United Way, that provided food, shelter, clothing, health services, social direction, adult education, employment services, and emergency health assistance to those in need—quite a task.

The Route One corridor south of Alexandria had a large population needing social services. Many of the people were from Mexico, Central America, Cuba, and Puerto Rico. Who better than a Spanish-speaking, recently retired, super-grade civil service officer to tackle the job?

Mrs. Kelso offered me a seat on the board of directors. The chairman of UCM was an Alexandrian attorney, Jerry Hyland, who was fluent in Spanish. He learned the language from his Puerto Rican wife. Jerry had run for county supervisor but didn't win. Two years later, he decided to run again. Bea and I decided to back him and work with him. We were sure he would be a good supervisor.

Jerry had enough standing in the community to be effective. Bea and I had lived in the area for five years and had been active in practically everything that went on. We were both well-known to the target voters: Latinos.

Shortly before the election, I wrote a letter to all those in the district with Hispanic surnames. I pointed out that this man understood and would fight for their rights and needs. It worked—Jerry was elected. It was good to be on the winning side, even if I wasn't the person getting elected. But soon that happened too, and Jerry was involved in that as well.

Jerry asked me to screen candidates for the board of education. There were seven candidates. I was asked to pick three I thought would be good to recommend to the county board of supervisors. I reported that I didn't see even one that I wanted to recommend, so he suggested I throw my hat into the ring. I ended up being one of the three finalists, and after a series of meetings with the supervisors, I was selected.

Then I had another job! I had made all the cuts and, in a sense, had won my first elected office. I was on a school board representing what the locals considered one of the nation's most prestigious school districts. To a large degree, I had responsibility for hundreds of thousands of kids in a couple dozen schools from elementary through high school.

I gleaned a bit of satisfaction from the knowledge that my selection to the school board would not have taken place a few years earlier. We were making progress after all. I like to think that my years of work as an educator had a lot to do with it.

Progress comes in small steps, however. The woman I replaced had been a longtime board member and was well liked. I'm sure she was very capable. I could almost feel the resentment from other board members. This was nothing new to me, and I was prepared for it. I knew just what to do—I buckled down and kept a polite, courteous, and not too aggressive manner.

One point I wanted to get across to the other board members was that although I was selected in large measure because of my understanding of the problems of Hispanics in my district, I intended to represent the entire community and act in the best interest of the entire community.

Apparently that shone through. After a while, I heard nothing more

FIGURE 18. Beatriz and Armando holding plaques of appreciation upon retiring from the Fairfax County, Virginia, School Board.

about how old so-and-so would have done things. I was now a full-fledged member of the board and was glad to have that part of the job behind me. Being a member of a large school board is hard enough without being part of any sort of bickering.

Although it took some effort, I visited every school and met with all the principals. They were the folks who had to solve the problems and board members were there to help them do that.

I also had a chance to get yet another look at this new educational phenomenon—computers. My work in Fairfax County, Virginia, complemented my work as a consultant for Hearst in New York City, San Francisco, and Bakersfield.

Altogether, being on the school board was an especially satisfying job. I was doing what I had trained for in college: educating kids. It was especially satisfying because the schools in Fairfax County were a microcosm of America, with kids of all races and economic groups. We had to keep them all functioning together.

When Bea and I decided to head back home to California, I wanted to ensure that my replacement was equally interested in the large number of Hispanic constituents. One lady seemed to fit the bill: Isis Castro. Isis and I had been friends for a long time. She was a very intelligent person, an educator who had worked for many years in elementary and secondary schools. In addition, she was a superb politician, an attribute as essential to being a school board member as being an educator was.

There were still other offers to keep me busy in my retirement. A Catholic priest, whose name I no longer remember, asked me to help fight the old problem of racial discrimination by serving on the board of directors of the United Catholic Conference for Justice, a group that was formed to fight injustice. Despite the fact that Hispanics were too often the target of injustice, no Hispanics seemed to want to get involved.

That was something I couldn't refuse to do. Education was my lifelong interest, and I was already up to my ears with so many different aspects of it. But racial injustice had also been my fight my entire life. So I took on yet another volunteer position as a member of the executive committee and soon hooked up with a wonderful gentleman—Jerry Ernest, a journalist.

Under Jerry's leadership, the United Catholic Conference for Justice was dedicated to bringing interracial coordination first within the church and then to the world outside the church. After three years, the auxiliary bishop Manuel Moreno of Washington DC was elected chairperson, and I was elected the bishop's alternate.

Being the bishop's alternate meant more work and more travel. Many of the trips were eye-popping, including one trip to Atlantic City. Being Catholics—especially Catholics on a Catholic junket—we went to Mass. The Mass we attended was held by a Hmong priest from the mountains of Vietnam. Protestants often tell me that the Roman Catholic ceremony is mystifying. The Hmong ceremony is mystifying to this Roman Catholic, but underneath, it is still the same ritual.

I once attended a national Catholic conference in Fargo, North Dakota, that was organized by Native Americans. I was surprised and sad to see how our Native Americans were living in poverty.

FIGURE 19. Coretta Scott King and Armando, 1984.

One other significant highlight from that time was meeting Mrs. Martin Luther King Jr. in Chicago. I was privileged to present her with a commendation for her work in human relations.

I also went to Atlanta, where I attended the elevation of my old co-chair Bishop Moreno to archbishop. It was an impressive ceremony. I have to point out, however, that I *did not attend* when he resigned under fire for mishandling a local scandal and witholding from authorities information regarding priests accused of pedophilia.

All that and I also made a trip to Russia—but that deserves a chapter of its own.

CHAPTER SIXTEEN

Capitalists in the Soviet Union, 1988–2001

I had no idea what lay ahead when I rang the doorbell of Randolph Hearst back in 1968. When Randy asked me in, I entered a different world—one I'd seldom visited before. And in return, Randy got a good look at my world. As a pop psychologist later termed it, it was a win-win situation.

Twenty years later, he showed me another world. I was already working on his computer study program when he called me. He was going to the Soviet Union on a junket to see how the Soviet Union handled bilingual education. It was a problem we had faced in the United States; ours involved mostly two languages, Spanish and English. Now he wanted to see if a country with many languages had answers we had overlooked.

The junket was the idea of Armand Hammer, MD, a mover and shaker par excellence, especially in the Soviet Union. He had been deeply involved with that country almost since the Bolshevik victory in the Russian Civil War in 1920. It didn't hurt a bit to have a man of Dr. Hammer's stature on our side.

Dr. Hammer was a capitalist and a staunch Republican. He was once convicted of illegally funding a Nixon campaign to the tune of thousands of dollars. He was later pardoned by President Ford. Although he was a capitalist, Hammer was a popular man in the Soviet Union. He had even lived in that country for a number of years and learned the language well enough to correct interpreters—as we learned on our tour.

Now, Randy and I were included in his international entourage. Like Hammer, most of the other members were capitalists. They were nabobs in international manufacturing of chemicals, metal (including aluminum), clothing, cans, and paper.

Randy had sent a letter to Vasili G. Zakharov, minister of cultural affairs of the Soviet Union, outlining our visit. The protocol was finished. Our trip would happen.

I would come face-to-face with the "evil empire" itself, and it was a vast one. The Union of Soviet Socialist Republics was a nation so vast it spanned nine time zones and needed six words in its name. I figured I'd better brush up a bit in order to know how to comport myself.

Fortunately, a couple teachers in the Fairfax School District helped me out. Both had taught in the Soviet Union as part of an exchange program. One taught at the primary and high school levels, and the other taught at the university level. I peppered them with questions of all sorts. For their part, they told me what to expect, what questions to ask, and what I should try to visit.

Their advice was wonderful. I wish I'd had the time and the ability to visit all the places they mentioned, but visiting someplace in the Soviet Union wasn't as easy as buying a ticket to Albuquerque.

We didn't go directly to the mysterious empire. Our first stop was the City of Lights, "Gay Paree" itself. This would not be my first visit, but Paris is Paris, always exciting and extremely expensive. That is why I booked a serviceable but definitely second-rate hotel.

Randy would have none of that. He immediately vetoed the idea. "Remember how I stayed in the same rooms as the rest of the folks on our cross-country trip in 1968? Now, it's quid pro quo time."

It's nice to be "forced" to do something you would really give your eyeteeth to do but won't because it's impractical. So I moved to the hotel where Randy was staying, the Ritz. Staying at a five-star hotel was an experience I could handle again—and again, and maybe even again. There's just something about indulging oneself!

We were in Paris three nights and I hit it lucky—I ate at a Bolivian restaurant and the owner set me up with a Bolivian expatriate taxi driver. I had my own tour guide, who spoke Spanish to boot! The driver and I used a different idiom here and there, and his Bolivian accent was a little out of sync with my Mexican/Barrio Logan Spanish, but it was much better than trying to cope with French, or even English with a French accent. Besides, the guy knew the City of Lights.

Finally, after three days of indulgence in Paris, I left with a group of twenty-one others in Dr. Hammer's private jet. We were off to Moscow.

Our first stop was a brief reception for Dr. Hammer in his suite in the Mezhdunarodnaya (no, I don't know what it means) Hotel. Here, too, we had accommodations far above average for the city. And for a good reason. Dr. Hammer had built the hotel, and then he gave it to the Russians. After the reception and a couple of reminders about how to comport ourselves, we were off to the Kremlin to meet with the prime minister of the Soviet Union and the chairman of the Council of Ministers (all one title for one person), Comrade Niryzhkov.

Dr. Hammer and his staff were received first. The Russians provided light refreshments while we bided our time for about an hour and a half. Dr. Hammer was obviously among friends in there.

When we were invited in, Dr. Hammer introduced Randolph Hearst. My friend described his corporation and his foundation, taking great care to emphasize our work with bilingual education and computer education. All this was, of course, the reason for our trip.

The prime minister was obviously interested. He spent a good half hour telling of how proud the Soviet Union was to have eliminated illiteracy. The upshot was that we would meet with the minister of culture, M. G. Zakharov, chairman of the state committee of education for the Soviet Union. At this point, Dr. Hammer interjected that Hearst was a giant in American publishing and television and radio. Our itinerary was immediately expanded to include a visit with a Mr. Nenashev, chairman of the state publishing committee of the Soviet Union. I wondered if anybody had a short title in the Soviet Union.

At the time of this junket, I was sixty-seven years old and was heartened to notice that Armand Hammer, at age ninety, had flown from Paris to Moscow, hosted a small reception, and met with high-level Russian diplomats for a good three hours while conversing in two very different languages—all in one day. He even corrected the translator on two occasions. I was beginning to believe that I might have quite a few years of productive life left in my old body. Today, at age eighty-six, I still think so.

FIGURE 20. *Left to right*: Veronica Hearst, (Unknown), Armand Hammer, Randolph Hearst, and Armando, 1988.

We had the weekend off. At the hotel I happened to run into an old friend, Elliott Richardson, who was in Moscow on business. Elliott had gained fame during the Watergate investigation by refusing Nixon's order to fire special prosecutor Archibald Cox, who was closing in on the details that would bring down the president. Elliott was fired, but unlike the guy who tried to enlist his aid in defying the law, he had a long and honorable government service. Elliott had been my boss at HEW. We chatted briefly and promised to look each other up when we got back to Washington.

On my free day, Saturday, I was tourist Mando. I changed my money into rubles and made sure I'd have some sort of laundry service. Then I took in Red Square, walked past the Kremlin, and spent some rubles on Bea in GUM, Moscow's huge department store. (*GUM*, by the way, is an abbreviation for six large words averaging ten letters.) That night, most of our entourage went to the Bolshoi Ballet. Afterward, Dr. Hammer hosted a dinner for all of us at the National Hotel.

When I got back to my hotel, a young lady in the lobby offered to accompany me to my room in exchange for some of my rubles. I, of course, declined. A visitor can handle only so much culture. Besides, tomorrow was Sunday, and I had to get up early to go to church.

The next morning I intended to go to Mass. I can honestly say that I have very seldom missed my Sunday obligation. I was sure the largest city in Europe, communist or not, would have a Catholic church somewhere, and some forty of them were listed in the tour guide. In a country of secrets, the location of a parish of the largest Christian religion in the world was a secret as far as I could tell. Nobody knew where an active church was.

Instead of going to Mass, I went with Randy and his wife Veronica to soak up some native culture. It was Moscow Day, the day the locals celebrated the founding of the city. We walked to a nearby park and took in a puppet show or two, some theater acts, band concerts, fashion shows, and dances. Somewhere along the way, our feet told us it had been a very busy weekend. The next day our real work would start. We headed back to the hotel.

On Monday morning we met with Vasili Zakharov, the Minister of Culture, and with G. A. Yagodin, the chairman of the state committee of education. Like me, Mr. Yagodin was interested in bilingual education. In the Soviet Union, curriculum changes were being proposed, foreign languages were being encouraged, and systems were being modified.

I think the ultimate story of education everywhere is change, change, change. It's necessary in a volatile world, and the Soviet Union was about as volatile as you could get. The rumblings had started, and in three years the Soviet Union would melt down and cease to exist in its current form, but that wasn't something we discussed. Our visit was to study education, not the future of a fading superpower.

Randy and I were interested primarily in bilingual and multilingual programs. Chairman Yagodin said his country had many places where they were facing the problem: the republics of Georgia, Kazakhstan, Armenia, and the Ukraine. He was especially proud of their efforts in Alma-Ata, former capital of Kazakhstan.

Ironically all the "republics" mentioned are now, at least technically, independent nations. We surely would visit one of them, but first we visited a couple of schools in Moscow. Our first stop was a kindergarten. I cannot vouch for whether this was an average school or a special showcase school. I'd guess the latter. Surely if the situation were reversed, I'd show off my best school. This Moscow kindergarten was a dandy. Medical care for the youngsters was provided by doctors and nurses on-site.

Their kindergarten was more extensive than ours, and kids as young as four attended that school. Promotion to first grade wasn't automatic upon their reaching age six; students had to take a test to see if they were capable of moving up to elementary school. I was reminded of the project I'd done for Hearst in New York, San Francisco, and Bakersfield.

Moscow schools and preschools (unlike most in America) were free for everyone. The one we visited was open from 7 a.m. to 7 p.m. in order to accommodate the parents who worked. If necessary, a child could stay overnight. What the school didn't accommodate was lazy students. The curriculum was a heavy one, and an effort was demanded from each student.

All in all, the school was well kept, pleasant, and safe, and it provided a good atmosphere for learning. As an old administrator, I was convinced from his answers that the director was well-informed and in touch with his school, its teachers, and its students.

Although I had gone to the Soviet Union to look at education, specifically bilingual education, I was a captive of Soviet bureaucracy. I wasn't free to move about as I wished because our hosts had scheduled meetings, luncheons, dinners, and even entertainment.

Our only chance to visit an elementary/secondary school was scheduled after the kindergarten visit. Thus, we arrived just as the school was letting out for the day. Nevertheless, we got a glimpse of an efficient, ambitious school. A thousand students were enrolled in grades one through ten, and they had sixty-eight teachers. My God! Any administrator in most American public schools would kill for a ratio like that—one teacher for every fifteen students!

The teachers were constantly kept on their toes. They had to be certified by a university and the state. They attended regular workshops. And the teachers, even the director, were subjected to an evaluation by parents, peers, directors, and central-office staff.

Schools in the Soviet Union were not totally different from those in the United States. The director we talked to said their problems were about like ours. The kids watched too much TV, smoked, and disrespected their teachers and parents.

Later we nearly scored a great public relations coup, but only nearly. Randy and the publishing committee chairman, Nenashev, discussed asking Raisa Gorbachev, the wife of Soviet President Mikhail Gorbachev, to write a piece about the schools in her country for some of the Hearst magazines. Nothing came of it, but in 1988 lots of things failed to come to fruition in that country. It was falling apart.

We also met with former Ambassador Anatoly Dobrynin, a man familiar to most Americans. Dobrynin, the man who President Kennedy and his staff worked with to avoid blowing the world to smithereens during the 1962 Cuban missile crisis, was now chairman of the Central Committee. He knew a lot about Hispanics in the United States and asked pertinent questions about bilingual education, especially bilingual education in the southwestern part of our country. Dr. Hammer pointed out that he himself was sponsoring some students from the University of Moscow while they were attending the University of New Mexico.

I felt our talks with Chairman Dobrynin were worth the trip. We were building friendship with the country that our country had once stood eyeball-to-eyeball with. The subject this time was kids, not nuclear weapons.

After the meeting, we went back to our rooms to freshen up, relax, and finally—after a day without much food—grab a bite to eat. Then we went back to Dr. Hammer's apartment for a reception for the same folks we'd just met and the American ambassador to the Soviet Union, Jack Matlock.

There I learned I would finally be free to roam about and inspect schools on my own, but not in Moscow. The rest of the party would head home the next day, but I would go to Alma-Ata, Kazakhstan, where I could get a look at bilingual education, Soviet style.

Before I left Moscow, I had a chance for one more tourist stop. Dr. Hammer used his considerable influence in Moscow to arrange a special visit—without standing in line for two hours—to visit Lenin's tomb. He did it so he could show his grandson the man he first met in

1921. I reflected that 1921 was the year Armando Rodriguez first made his appearance in Gomez Palacio, Mexico.

When I was waiting in the hotel lobby for my ride to the airport, I met Mike Tyson. We had a friendly chat and I got his autograph. Mike, a rather taciturn fellow, didn't exactly talk my ear off. In fact, I'm glad he left my ear alone altogether.

It's three thousand miles from Moscow to Alma-Ata, a relatively short hop in the Soviet Union, but one that would take you across the entire United States. Short hop or not, traveling in that police state wasn't easy. It took a visa, airline reservations, hotel reservations, and permission to meet with people—in this case, school officials. Thank heaven for the influence of Dr. Hammer. His staff took care of everything.

Kazakhstan is a virtual laboratory for the examination of multilingual education. Its eighteen million people include more than one hundred different cultural groups. More than three million students attend nine thousand schools.

Much of this I saw in the beautiful and friendly capital, Alma-Ata. After an overnight flight I was met by my guide and interpreter, Saida Erlepesova. Saida was an English professor at the city's Institute of Languages. She was accompanied by the director of programs for the republic and his assistant.

After a short respite and a bite to eat at my hotel, I was whisked away to meet the deputy minister of education for the Republic of Kazakhstan, Mirzatal Dzholdaspekov. He and his staff would accompany me on my visits to the child-care centers and the elementary/secondary schools. Quite an entourage, but this *was* the Soviet Union.

The first stop was a child-care center and a kindergarten where we were met by children in their native Turkish costumes. After the children gave us flowers, we met the director who explained the program, which was much the same as in Moscow, except Kazakh was the primary language, and Russian was the secondary language. Kazakh is derived from Turkish.

Next we visited a number of elementary/secondary schools where I was shown classes in language, art, math, science, carpet weaving (the traditional art of the region), and physical education. I was treated to an assembly where students from seven to sixteen performed not only in Kazakh and Russian, but in English as well. They also recited poems, sang songs, played instruments, and danced. In the finale, everybody in the hall held hands and sang, in English, the song so often heard at protests throughout the United States: "We Shall Overcome." The theme of the presentation was peace, and peace was stressed at every stop. It was proclaimed with decorations, bulletin boards, and activities.

It was emotional, and I got caught up in it. Sure, it was just words being sung, but the idea of peace was coming from the mouths of children who someday would be running the country. Those kids are now about thirty. I wonder if they remember the bright promise of the future. Even if they are still in Kazakhstan, they live in a different country than the one I visited.

Later, I was escorted to the cultural center for more folk dancing and singing by performers wearing local costumes. They were a versatile group. The assistant spoke not only English, Kazakh, and Russian, but Spanish as well.

We visited the Children's Palace, sponsored by the Communist Party. Such palaces could be found throughout the Soviet Union. They are designed for children ages ten to fifteen.

I had a chance to meet and talk with the governing committee of students, which was composed of junior and high school kids. A terrific audience, they were very interested in talking about their counterparts in my country. They were especially interested in me because their concept of Americans was gleaned mostly from television—and I didn't look like John Wayne.

The misconception goes both ways. We have heard so much about the dreaded "Russkies" that it is a bit disconcerting to look at young kids and realize that they would fit in at an American junior or senior high school.

As for the John Wayne misconception, I explained that America, like Russia, comprises many races. We strived, and sometimes succeeded, to treat all equally. When we failed as individuals, laws were passed requiring equal treatment. Even as I spoke, I reflected that I, a guy called Shadow in a land of light-haired giants, was a good example of how our society works, sometimes in spite of ourselves.

I spent only a couple of days in Alma-Ata, but it seemed like an entire year. I was busy going from school to school to cultural center and finally to an ice-skating stadium that was the pride of Kazakhstan. My interpreter and escort stayed with me so much that I felt she was my shadow. (Imagine Shadow having a shadow.) Still, unlike in Moscow, I was free to move about as much as I wished. And I was grateful to Saida Erlepesova for her help in all respects. I hope she's doing well under the new independent regime in Kazakhstan.

Although we didn't discuss it once, freedom from Mother Russia was on its way. Two years earlier, young Kazakhs had demonstrated in Alma-Ata. Two years after my visit, Kazakhstan's independence would be secured.

The movement toward independence may have accounted for my freedom to move about, or it may have just been that we were so far from the seat of power. In any case, my role there was certain. I was there as a guest of the Soviet Union. My function was to study bilingual and multilingual education. That's what I had to stick to.

After a whirlwind two and one-half days, I packed my bags and flew back to Moscow. There I had to endure the usual paperwork. And then I went home.

CHAPTER SEVENTEEN

Christy and Roddy

Bea and I figured we'd have a large family, practically a tradition in Catholic, Mexican American families. Our first child arrived almost simultaneously with my diploma from San Diego State. I missed my graduation to stay home and help Bea when Ruth Christine added herself to the family.

Bea had my personal help, mostly limited to sympathy, plus the help of the hospital staff because it was a difficult delivery. The doctor said my wife couldn't have any more kids. That was it; we'd have to settle for having a small family. That wouldn't be a particular problem because we could love one kid just as much as a half dozen. Christy made it easy to love. She was, and still is, a lovely daughter. With just a small family and no prospects of a larger one, we continued living in the apartment we rented from Bea's mom for a couple of years, and then we bought a house—a small one.

Our family expanded, but not with more children. It expanded with animals, thanks in part to Paul Walker. Paul was a retired navy chief, and I knew him as a wrestling referee. At that time, he ran the Dog Motel in La Jolla. It was a place to board dogs for people who were traveling. Sometimes, after being away from their pets for a while, folks realized just how much trouble their critters were and decided that they could get along without them after all. They just wouldn't come back to the Dog Motel to claim them.

That might have been a solution for the vacationers, but not for the dogs or Paul himself. He loved animals and had to find a home for them. In one such case, Paul saw a solution to his problems. Bea and I loved pets, and Christy, who was about a year old by then, obviously "needed a cuddly dog." Sure enough, he had one we could rescue from whatever fate befalls dogs left behind in boarding houses. We adopted Mike, a dachshund, usually referred to as a sausage hound.

Mike didn't last too long at our home. Christy loved him, hugged him, and dragged him around. Then she developed welts, and we blamed the animal. Back he went, with the hope that someone, somewhere, wouldn't be allergic to him and would give him a good home. Later, we discovered it wasn't the dog's fault at all: Christy had a general allergy unrelated to dogs. Back we went to the Dog Motel, but Mike had moved on, whatever that meant. We didn't ask for details.

But Paul, like all good chief petty officers, had another solution. He had another abandoned dog, a beagle named Smokey. We were moving up in size—and in noise if Smokey decided to bay at the moon. Those beagles can be noisy. Later Christy added several cats, all black and white, and all named Smokey. Life can be simple for kids.

After we moved out of our apartment and into our own home, we added some farm animals to our family, but Christy figured they were pets. That's why we didn't go into any details when a duck that had been there one day wasn't there the next—not when we would have to explain what was for supper that night. Now, a half century later, I suppose she's figured it out.

As our menagerie grew, so did our family. Convinced our family was limited to only three (not counting four-legged critters), we hired a contractor to build us our own home, a small one. Then, within a year, we outgrew it. On April 14, 1953, Roddy, AKA Roderick Christopher Rodriguez, checked in and took up residence in our small house.

We moved to bigger digs, the one dubbed Rod's Little Acre by my friend and fellow teacher Henry Wiggins. There we had more room to play and more room for our animals. Christy loved her little brother about as much as she did her cats, but he just wasn't as furry or as pretty.

I think it's a rule that in a two-child family, the kids will be as different as day and night. Christy and Roddy differed in both temperament and the ambition to excel in school. Although both Bea and I were Catholics, and Bea had gone to parochial schools, we enrolled both of our children in public schools. That was the way I wanted it. I was a product of public schools and, more important, an employee of them.

I don't think it would have mattered where Christy went; she was going to do well in the classroom and with her friends. She worked hard, never caused any problems, and got good grades.

Roddy was a different story. Excelling in grades just wasn't at the top of his list. While this usually didn't endear him to teachers, he showed an ability to get by. Just getting by wasn't what we had in mind. It just doesn't work in a competitive society, especially for a minority kid.

But he was a natural-born charmer, and he used his charm for all it was worth. By the time he was in the fourth grade, he had perfected his art to the point where we felt he was simply getting by with almost everything. As a teacher and a vice-principal, I felt this was unacceptable.

I wanted confirmation of Roddy's abilities, so I asked Joe Tody, the school district psychologist, to test our son. Joe concluded that Roddy could, indeed, do better, and he encouraged us to work with him and settle for nothing short of his best.

To get the added discipline our son needed, I turned my back on my own school system and turned to the one run by my church. We enrolled Roddy in Saint John of the Cross, a parochial school in Lemon Grove. He stayed there until we moved north to work in the Pat Brown administration.

Growing up is tough enough no matter where it's done, and we worried about our two kids. Our life didn't make it easy for them, with our moving so often and their having to adjust to new friends and often a new curriculum at each stop. And their dad didn't have just a job. I was often either trying to get elected or trying to help someone else in my party get elected. That meant that just about half their friends' parents disliked me, or at least my politics.

But politics it was, and our kids jumped in right alongside Bea and me. When I was campaigning, they walked the precinct door-to-door with me—even when they were little kids.

As they got older, they did things like telephoning to get out the vote, distributing campaign literature, and putting out signs. They were involved in just about everything that goes on in a political campaign. One way or another, politics was part of their lives on a local, state, and national level.

I now worry that we pushed them to be adults ahead of their time. How traumatic was it for them to learn that everybody doesn't even have to pretend to like a politician? I have to wonder about the effect of all those doors slammed in our faces.

But they grew up, each stage an adventure for them and for us. Christy was a senior and Roddy was in junior high when I was called to Sacramento. Governor Pat Brown named me director of the Bureau of Intergroup Relations, and we moved to nearby Davis.

The change was especially rough on Christy, who had planned on finishing high school with her friends at Mount Miguel High and then going on to one of the local colleges with them. Now she was nearly five hundred miles from her friends. All this was happening at a time when her childhood was ending, and she was trying to cope with becoming a young woman.

And the five hundred miles became three thousand. Within a year, I got the call from Washington to join the Johnson administration. Roddy, we could take along, but Christy wanted nothing to do with moving yet again, especially to a completely different part of the country. She wanted to go to college in her hometown, preferably to the University of California, San Diego.

That worked out fine. Many of her friends from Mount Miguel High were going to UCSD, and it was emerging as one of the top schools in the state. So it was UCSD for our daughter, while the rest of us were off to work for the president.

After about a year, we got a call from the school counselor who told us that Christy needed help. Her attention was diverted from her studies, and she wasn't doing well academically. As one who got a big boost in politics by rebelling against the President of the United States, I was not one to deny our eldest child the right, even the duty, to rebel.

And she *was* rebelling, big time. Mentored by activists like Angela Davis and Carlos Blanco, our daughter had become a student activist, advocating for civil rights and greater opportunities for students of color and opposing the war in Vietnam. As a founding member of UCSD MEChA, Christy soon extended her activities beyond campus.

UCSD was emerging as one of the top schools in the state, and although it was becoming a liberal institution that tolerated extreme positions, it tolerated no deviation from the pursuit of knowledge. That meant Christy had to buckle down and study. And that was *not* what she was doing.

Our dream of raising two well-educated children was in jeopardy. Bea and I returned to San Diego to talk face-to-face with both our daughter and her counselor. We thought things got better after that, and I'm sure they did.

Still, things happen no matter what. About a year later, Christy called with more news—she was pregnant and she didn't want to get married. Her pregnancy wasn't exactly in our plans either, but we were pleased that she took a mature view of it. Perhaps best of all, we were glad she had decided to have the baby and trusted us enough to confide in us.

We asked her to come to Virginia and live with us until she had her baby. On January 14, 1971, Armando Simon Rodriguez, named after his grandfather and great grandfather, joined the family. Christy and little Mando stayed with us for three years, and during that time, Christy worked at various jobs.

Then, the father of an old school friend offered her a job near Oakland. A chance to return home to California! She drove back and lived there until I got work at East Los Angeles College. She moved in with us again and worked in Long Beach.

In the meantime, Roddy was growing up as well. He had graduated from Mount Vernon High School as a good, but not spectacular, scholar. He wanted to go to college near his old stomping grounds. With our blessing, Roddy enrolled at the United States International University, a highly respected school with a beautiful campus overlooking the Pacific in San Diego's Point Loma.

And he did well, if not spectacularly, in college. He seemed to thrive in his old hometown. Like so many San Diego kids, he was a surfer. He perfected that sport while chasing an education. He wanted to be a teacher. I bore up well under the surfing and was pleased with his choice of a career path. We will always need educators in this country.

Alas, after three years he headed north to take a summer job in the

San Joaquin Valley, probably because an old girlfriend from Mount Vernon High School was up north. He eventually finished his education of California State University, Fullerton. Our family now had a second-generation college graduate!

Not long after Roddy's graduation, we added a couple of new family members. Roddy was living at home while attending Cal State, Fullerton. He was still dating Barbara Kline, who was his high school sweetheart and the daughter of an army colonel. Barbara had been working, at least indirectly, at East Los Angeles College.

Before long, just like Bea and me, Roddy and Barbara were married in Our Lady of Guadalupe Church, right off the I-5 freeway in Barrio Logan. This was followed by a big reception at the officers' club at the Naval Air Station, North Island.

Roddy's wedding may have been in a church, but the marriage wasn't made in heaven. He and Barbara had two children, Miguel and Nicolas, but it was all over in a few years. Roddy kept the kids and later married again.

About eight years ago, Roddy married Liana Spring, a coworker he met at John Wayne Airport in Orange County. They live close enough to visit, and we get to see Miguel and Nicolas.

Like Roddy, Christy had marital problems. She met Tom Blackburn while we were still living in Whittier, and she was working in Long Beach. And like the rest of us, Tom and Christy were married at Our Lady of Guadalupe. They had a son and named him after the famous Mexican general Emiliano Zapata.

Tom was an entrepreneur of sorts, a fellow with lots of ideas, but none that paid off well. He and his family were often a bit short in the bank account. When Bea and I moved back to Washington to work for Jimmy Carter, Christy and Tom also moved back to that area. The marriage broke up not long after.

The hard part about writing one's history is that it has to be fact, not fiction, so everything doesn't come out as well as an hour-long TV drama or even a well-crafted book. For all our efforts, we are not perfect. But the best part of my story is that it's about my family, and we all love and support each other whether everybody fits neatly into the "proper" niche or not.

Bea and I have two wonderful kids, four grandsons, and a great grandson, Armando Rafael Rodriguez—Mandito. Best of all, we are still in love with each other and celebrate it every day.

We remain close with our extended family. Together we keep alive a grand Mexican tradition, Las Posadas. This is a Christian celebration that originated in Latin America. It depicts Mary and Joseph looking for shelter after fleeing from Herod's edict to kill all young children of Israel. They were turned away from several inns before they found shelter.

The pageant in our family has been modified to accommodate changing times, changing attitudes, and the automobile. Las Posadas has always been a movable feast where, originally, folks walked from house to house. But that would be difficult in our case because not everybody lives within walking distance. Our Posada takes places in four homes, one of which is forty miles from one of the others. Thank heaven for the automobile.

Participation isn't limited to our family. It includes friends and friends' friends and almost anybody who wishes to come along. Sometimes as many as fifty, maybe even a hundred, people show up. We start at my house in El Cajon at 5:30 on a Saturday evening about a week before Christmas. The entire group is divided into two parts: one half represents the Holy Family, the other, the innkeepers. The innkeepers are inside; the family, outside. Each member of each group has a song sheet. Those in the family ask for shelter. The innkeepers explain there is no room. Then the family is invited in. That's not quite like in the Bible, but that's the way we do it.

About an hour later, everybody arrives at the second house, usually my niece Elisa Sanchez's house in Del Cerro. This time the roles are reversed, and the ritual is about the same except that we have light dessert and salad.

Then it's on to Dora Castallenos's house in Paradise Hills for the main course featuring menudo. Finally we head back to Spring Valley to the home of Irma Castro for more dessert.

Food, drink, games, and merrymaking at all stops. At Dora's house, where we have the main menu, we include a piñata—a grand tradition. Some folks don't make it all the way around for one reason or another, and others join in late. It doesn't matter. The biggest benefit is that folks get together and enjoy each other's company.

Bea and I also host a family get-together on Christmas and invite other friends over to a New Year's Day open house. These traditions are becoming more important to us. I was reminded of that recently when the surgeons removed a large section of my cancerous intestine. While I'm still charging ahead, I find nostalgia to be more important than ever.

CHAPTER EIGHTEEN

My Final Retirement
(So Far), 2006–7

An old American proverb says that if you have something important to do, give the job to a busy boy. It would have been easy in 1983 to just walk away from my job and seek that well-earned rest, but my attempt at retirement was a failure. I ended up with more jobs than I'd had as a young man trying to finish college and start a family.

I tried again to retire in 1991, and again I failed. But, to tell the truth, this "failure" doesn't bother me one bit. A fellow who spent a lifetime working, often at two or three jobs, just can't quit—not even to play golf.

I like golf, and I'm pretty good at it too. Athletic things came easy to me, especially long ago, or so it seems after all these years. While we lived in Virginia, I had a decent handicap and even turned in a par round every so often. I've been playing the game for a long time now. Bob Dowdy taught me how to play at the city's nine-hole course in Balboa Park back in 1939.

Now, despite being retired and having a good knack for the game, I still consider myself merely a weekend golfer. Oh, I suppose if you press me, I'll tell you about the two times I made a hole in one.

I insist golf is merely a pastime, not some all-consuming task. I hung out with the wrong crowd to be content to immerse myself in the world of leisure. The people who inspire me are the very folks who never wake up wondering, "Oh, what will I do today," not even long after they retired.

Armand Hammer didn't look much like a fellow just taking it easy when, at age ninety, he headed up a tour of the Soviet Union for a group of visiting businesspeople and educators. My friend and former congressman Lionel Van Deerlin, at ninety-three, is still involved in about every sort of political activity going on in San Diego County. Furthermore, he still writes a weekly column for the *San Diego Union-Tribune*. He recently missed his first deadline in twenty-seven years. That took a heart attack, but he was back in print a mere two weeks later.

Compared to Van and me, Charlie Erickson is a kid—merely in his mid-seventies—but he has been slowed down by an illness and can't use both hands. Still, he is usually in his office at the *Hispanic Link* when I call. He manages to do as much with one hand as most folks do with two. Charlie simply uses his head more than his hands, something we all should try.

Until his death a few weeks ago, Dean Bistline was often busy taking care of a 102-year-old woman. Some fourteen years earlier, he got involved with a San Francisco group called Friends of the Elderly. A few years younger than I, Dean said he would start acting his age and taking it easy when I do. I hope he never did.

My old boss Jimmy Carter may not go down in history as the greatest American president. I think that was just the luck of the draw, because greatness is too often foisted on us by circumstances. I do think Carter will go down in history as the best ex-president.

Scarcely a year goes by without that octogenarian writing a book, espousing a noble cause, receiving a peace prize, or getting his calloused hands dirty with Habitat for Humanity. The current president, after initially ignoring Hurricane Katrina, finally showed up for many photo ops. By the time Bush got to the hurricane-damaged areas, Carter was already there pounding nails.

And so it goes. I could name hundreds of folks who keep going long after the "normal" retirement age of sixty-five. All have one thing in common—they worked hard their entire lives and did not stop because of their gray hair or shortened steps. That described me when I left government service in 1983. I didn't get to "enjoy" what I suspect is a dubious pleasure—being nonproductive. A relatively high-level civil servant who was well-known in the community and who spoke the language of a large minority group was in demand. I was busy for the next eight years.

At age seventy I would once again leave the rat race of Washington and see what retirement might mean in tranquil San Diego. With so many ties to San Diego, we felt we belonged there and decided to move back. It was a sad trip. Bea and I had made so many friends in Washington, and we had been involved in so many important events. What awaited me in San Diego? Somehow I suspected it wouldn't involve a pipe and slippers.

We picked out a house in El Cajon, some fifteen miles from Barrio Logan, where Bea and I had grown up. As usual, we had a lot of work to do. The house was beautiful and well maintained, but now it was ours. I'm fussy; Bea doubly so. We changed things. We dug out the plants that were merely decorative and replaced them with trees, bushes, and cacti that bore fruit.

Did you know that the paddles of some cactus plants are delicious? They are called *nopales*, and we learned to eat them in the days when there wasn't always enough money to buy groceries from the market. They are still delicious, but now we can pick them from our own cactus stand in the backyard—but don't tell anybody.

This and that, moving things here and there, it's a never-ending task. Now, fourteen years after we returned to San Diego, we're still moving things around. I do play golf weekly and still shoot within spitting distance of par. Bea still whomps younger ladies in her weekly tennis games.

In San Diego, as in Virginia, I immediately found myself busy with the sort of work that has an impact on other people's lives. For ten years after moving back home, I continued my efforts with Randy Hearst on his computer program. It ceased only after he died and the money dried up.

Before I left Virginia, I had joined the San Diego High School Alumni Association. By the time Bea and I moved back here, the association had set up a foundation to raise money for scholarships and projects to improve the quality of education and extracurricular activities. I joined and did what I could to help.

Wrestling had been my sport at San Diego High School, and more than fifty years later, I got involved with it again when I helped raise some money for uniforms. It wasn't a problem. I just called Tom Pine, one of the old wrestlers, and that was that—the wrestlers were duly outfitted.

Then, as would seem appropriate, the sport I'd been so involved with led me to another task, and this one was more personal. My high school coach Frank Crosby taught me how to wrestle, and he taught me so much about life. I stayed in contact with him as long as he lived. Now I had a chance to honor my old coach and help the sort of kids I'd spent a lifetime trying to help.

The alumni association had established the Frank Crosby Award, a cause Coach Crosby would have approved of. The award was set up to encourage underachievers who were showing promise—to help them keep improving. Nothing could have honored the old coach more. I was proud to work on a committee that recognized him.

Appropriately enough, in retirement I did just as I had in "real life"—after I'd worked for a high school, I moved up to college. A couple of years after I returned to the San Diego area, President Thomas Day of San Diego State University invited me to serve on his advisory committee. Little old San Diego State College was now San Diego State University, a huge and prestigious institution.

In 1996, when Dr. Steve Weber replaced Day, he dubbed us the Ambassadors to San Diego State University. We ambassadors still give advice to the president, but at least once a year, some of us make the trip to Sacramento. That's the seat of power for California and my old stomping grounds. One might surmise that my having been so heavily involved in politics has something to do with my being frequently tapped for the trips to our state capital. Some say it's lobbying, and I suppose it is. But we are trying to keep our university among the best in the country.

Not all projects became a resounding success. About a year ago, Dr. Weber asked me to help him start a program suggested by a college in Tijuana. The idea seemed great, but the timing was impractical. The Mexicans wanted to initiate an international exchange program with their students and our students attending college classes in each other's countries.

It was a great idea, but it was a bad time to consider anything that involved crossing the border. It hasn't improved a bit, and I don't see any changes coming soon. Still, it deserved study. I attended a full-blown program in Tijuana and promised to offer whatever help I could.

My nephew Carlos Rodriguez-Rubio is a professor at a university in Tijuana and at the United States International University. In addition, he is a part-time instructor at San Diego State. I introduced him to Dr. Weber. The program, while it has great merit, is in limbo, and I'm afraid it'll be held off for a few years.

An earlier program had started out well and then seemed to die out. A science professor at San Diego State University wanted to help minority students, primarily Hispanic and African American, qualify for admission to prestigious universities, especially Ivy League schools. This ambitious program involved tutoring and lots of money.

And, as you might guess, I got Randy Hearst involved once again. My friend opened up the Hearst Foundation's purse strings, and the program got off the ground. All the students in the program made it into a college science program, although not all made it into the likes of Yale or Harvard. In any case, it sure was a success, but for some reason, it was discontinued.

After my retirement, I received my second honorary doctorate. This one had its beginnings from my work in President Lyndon Johnson's administration. I wrote earlier about three fellows who helped National Hispanic University get off the ground. Early in my stint with Johnson, I received a request from these three fellows from the San Francisco area. They were well-educated Mexican Americans who were living the good life, but who wanted to do something to make life better for their fellow Hispanics.

They asked me to help them establish a bilingual consulting firm in the Bay Area. This was right in line with my job at the time. I checked them out and helped, mostly by finding funds for their project. It worked and it grew, eventually becoming a four-year college housed in a San Jose barrio community.

The history of my life is one of always striving to make it up the ladder one more step. I always hoped to help others—especially other Latinos—do the same. If I was successful in this, it was because so many people quite unlike me helped. A list of those who went out of their way to help me would include many who weren't Hispanic and many who had few connections to Hispanics.

After accumulating friends for eighty-six years, I cannot possibly acknowledge everybody who kept me from falling on my face, or worse. I apologize to those I may have overlooked, but I must mention some.

Dean Bistline and I hailed from different countries but had somewhat similar backgrounds. I came from the agricultural area of central Mexico, Dean, from the corn belt of Iowa. We both taught at Samuel Gompers Junior High and shared political philosophies. Best of all, we liked each other. When I jumped into politics, Dean came along. I called on Dean to keep me out of trouble in almost every major job I had. If I get credit for anything in my life, the most credit would have to be shared with Dean (except for catching that girl who lived across the street!).

Randolph Hearst was in and out of my life from 1968 until his death in 2001. If I accomplished anything outside of government, it was mostly due to my friend Randy and the Hearst Foundation. Our relationship was much more than a business relationship. We were good friends, and we grew old together. A few months before his death, we talked about the tribulations of growing old. He had suggested that we have the hunks of skin hanging from our chins removed. He thought they looked like wattles on a turkey.

Our friendship lasted longer than his marriages. I remember the day Veronica, his third wife, called to tell me he had died suddenly from a heart attack. She picked me, a longtime friend, to share her grief. I did, indeed. We both wept as we talked.

I waited in vain for an invitation to his funeral. I wanted to say good-bye to an old friend. It didn't come, nor have I heard a thing from her or Randy's family since.

I started life as a Mexican born in Gomez Palacio, Mexico. In San Diego's Barrio Logan, I became a Chicano, Latino, sometimes a spic, and often worse. I earned my citizenship by serving in the army of my adopted country. Somewhere along the line, I became known as a Mexican American. Many years of government service made me an American! Now I am a bona fide Mexican again.

I've always felt a kinship with the land of my birth, so I was especially pleased when Christy named her second child after a Mexican hero, General Zapata. Bea and I have always made frequent trips to

Mexico. Then, about the time I was president of East Los Angeles College, we bought a time-share condo there.

Ownership of property in Mexico is somewhat of a problem for foreigners. Someone pointed out that we would have several advantages if we simply reapplied for Mexican citizenship, which I thought I'd relinquished when I became a U.S. citizen in 1943.

Amazingly, it was simple, and it was legal. In 2001 I simply offered proof of my place of birth and our marriage certificate to the Mexican consul, and it was done. Bea and I both have what is called dual citizenship. I'm a Mexican and an American, but any overt act of being a Mexican would jeopardize my U.S. citizenship. I promise not to vote south of the border—not even if it's close.

Still, at age eighty-six, I have come almost full circle. I'm a citizen of two countries I love, and I'm proud of both.

Index